FROM BROKEN NECK TO BROKEN RECORDS

A Masters Cyclist's Guide to Winning

Rose Marie Ray, Author

Sandy Scott, Co-Author

From Broken Neck to Broken Records
A Masters Cyclist's Guide to Winning

Library of Congress 1-244079116, 9/14/09

ISBN: 978-0-9629361-1-1

Yankee Publishing, Seminole, Florida 33776

Cover Photographs by Mark Estrada

Graphic Design by Nieves Rivas, Creative FX

To The Children

Pamela Ray Chancey and Ian Ray

Kimberly Sadowsky Bush, Chris and Evan Scott

In Loving Memory

Sanford "Sandy" David Sadowsky, Jr.

He left us too soon without realizing
the potential of his great athleticism.

*We have passed on to you the genetics for
athletics from the generations that have
preceded us. It is the gift of life that will never
let you down and we hope you will use it well.*

CONTENTS

CHAPTER 32...

...

PREFACE

The story of Sandy Scott and his broken neck and broken records is becoming legendary. His might-be-considered miraculous survival of a broken neck suffered on October 30, 2005, has been circulated around the globe via Internet interviews, blogs, Facebook, Twitter, and other media. Photographs taken of him winning his post-recovery races have been on the covers of sports magazines and in newspapers and have won awards because they convey the determination and grit of Sandy racing to the finish line.

It is a huge story of success and triumph and never saying "I can't do it!" when all was thought to be lost and the physicians and surgeons could not believe he was walking, talking, and riding his trainer in the garage.

I shared Sandy's nearly catastrophic injury from the first thought when it happened of, "Oh my God, he must be dead" to helping find the spinal surgeon who would make a difference in his life. It was inspirational to see him learn enough about his injury to be his own personal spinal consultant. Between the bouts of depression and pain, his determination to get back to cycling and racing was undeterred.

Sharing this story became my imperative and I started the book when Sandy made his comeback, record-breaking, gold-medal win in a 5K time trial at the State of Florida, Senior Games in 2006. Beginning with the award of "AMS Masters Comeback Athlete of the Year" for 2007, from Masters Athlete Magazine and the radio interview by GrowingBolder.com on WFLA, Florida, and ending on the podium where he won his 11th state championship gold medal in the State of Florida, United States Cycling Federation, 20K Time Trial, the story has taken on a bigger-than-life aura as has Sandy.

Thanks to all of those who have responded to Sandy's story and his training blogs for Masters Cycling & Masters Athlete magazines that run on both MastersCycling.com and Masters-Athlete.com. It shows that there are a great many masters athletes who have similar stories to share and adhere to the "Scott Method" of training and winning— the enhanced version of which we are presenting in this book.

We know that you can benefit from Sandy's vast knowledge of cycling and training methods and all of the other information we have included in the book. It will show you the way to be a good cyclist, a competitor, and/or a winner of medals if you work hard and take your training to new levels. Whether you are 40 or 90 years old, if you are competing, you are a winner!

Thanks to family, friends, and cyclists from all over the world who have encouraged us in this endeavor. Special thanks to Bill Shafer, co-founder of the GrowingBolder.com network for his unrelenting support and encouragement and Sean Callahan of Masters Athlete Magazine for recognizing Sandy and all of the other extraordinary masters athletes in the USA., and, last but not least, Sandy's generous product sponsors: Guru Bicycles, Montreal, Canada, Outspokin Bicycles, Clearwater, FL, Pirate Gear, Hamburg, Germany, and Teschner Technologies Group, Queensland, Australia.

May the wind always be at your back when racing to the gold medal.

Rose Marie Ray

INTRODUCTION

What is it that makes a super athlete? Is it only the genetics passed down through families that makes a person a breaker of records and winner of gold medals? If you were to meet Sandy in a room full of athletic people, you might, by a long shot, pick him out as the #1 competitor in masters cycling in the State of Florida and the terror of the fast peloton rides several times a week in St. Petersburg. What we look like especially when dressed in everyday clothing does not always correlate to what we can do in athletics. It is not only genetics and how we use them, but our individual wealth of other traits that makes us unique in all we do, especially in athletics.

This is the age of "masters" athletes—35 years plus and those of us who may be retired or working at jobs that do not require us to be in an office from 9:00AM to 5:00PM. We are having the time of our lives as we take every opportunity to get out and swim, run, or bike—or do all three and, perhaps, make time for a round of golf in the late afternoon.

There are many of us you see around town wearing tee shirts with "Senior Games" or "Iron Man" or, perhaps, "U.S.A. National Team, Senior Olympics." We may have wrinkles and weathered skin along with our white hair, but we are a force in athletics today all over the world. Some of us may have pacemakers or defibrillators embedded in our chests, but we are seasoned athletes with athletic hearts who love to compete. "Age is only a number" I've heard it, and I believe it!

The first part of the book is the extraordinary story of an outstanding cyclist and how he was suddenly told that he would never ride a bicycle again. It is about a methodical plan to solve an enormous, life-threatening problem that required faith, hope, and a lot of luck.

The second part of the book is a "how to" for all of the athletes who need a mentor, a guide, or a talented coach who can lead them to the podium and, on the way, perhaps break some records.

Sanford "Sandy" Scott is one of many super athletes who started bicycling later in life. It became a passion with him and he now spends most of the day working at his job of riding one of his several bikes. How he got to be a highly-visible masters athlete was through a series of events triggered by a nearly catastrophic cycle racing accident.

Stories abound about people who have become athletes late in life to solve depression, boredom, or to fulfill a need for a new lifestyle. We meet the most interesting people as we compete, but we do not know the how, where, and why they got so caught up in athletics. Sandy was a seasoned runner for many years so it was an easy transition for him.

I need to tell you a few things about him and where he came from—important facts for all the chosen few who are recorded in the athletic history books. For us and our children, he is a man to be emulated. There is a special something in a person like Sandy that allowed him to use his brains and brawn to overcome adversity. He is not your average run-of-the-mill kind of athlete, but distinctly independent and determined to make every day wonderful while racing around on two wheels. His personal history is rich in the independent spirit and intellectual always waiting for some new challenge to take on. It starts the same in all of us: what we do as children, and who we had to follow and those that took us under their wings and nurtured us into the adults we became.

Sandy was born in New York City and raised in Stockton, California. As an only child for most of his youth, Sandy occupied himself with playing competitive chess, reading a lot of books—not novels for the most part--and opened his horizons to the world via short-wave radio. The radio was his world vision from his bedroom and where he began his insatiable desire to always be learning and challenging his innate curiosity. He had a couple of close friends who shared his passion for knowledge and they pursued music, competitive chess, sports, computers, and adventures until he was in his mid-thirties.

His father, although he had no direct contact with Sandy for most of his life, competed in football, basketball, and track. He passed on his terrific genes for athletics to Sandy who is built for speed: all muscle and bone with a tiny bit of fat. But, as we said earlier, that did not give him the courage and grit he needed to succeed in masters athletics.

Although he has a Mensa-class mind, Sandy nearly flunked his senior year of high school out of shear boredom. Because his mother went in to see the school's principal and pled his case, he was given a chance to pass all of his final exams and graduated with his class of 1957. He was 17 years old. His mother, an artist and intellectual, was convinced that he was unprepared to go to college, and insisted that he join the military.

Sandy spent two-years-plus of his four-year enlistment in the Navy. After electronics school, he got assigned to a destroyer that patrolled the Straits of Formosa. During the crisis between China and Formosa, the Mainland Chinese shelled the offshore islands of Quemoy and Matsu and had fire-control radar constantly aimed at his patrolling ship. He and his ship mates lived on the edge as they were told that, if hostilities were to break out between the US and China, they would have a survival time of 30-seconds. That certainly gave new meaning to his life.

He tested for, passed the exams, and was accepted into the Naval Reserve Officer Training Corps, and received a fleet appointment to the U.S. Naval Academy, Annapolis. However, the timing was not right to begin Annapolis immediately and he was anxious to get on with his life so he accepted an NROTC scholarship to the University of Kansas. He got married; had children; and became a motorcycle police officer for the city of Palo Alto, California, and ultimately finished his college via the University of California-Berkeley; St. Johns University, and Embry-Riddle Aeronautical University where he graduated with a degree in Aeronautical Engineering.

Sandy found his ultimate job and his first passion in life when he went to work flying airplanes for Eastern Airlines. After 25 years, he had risen to the "top dog" position in the airline industry as captain/check airman/examiner when they went out of business. The loss of flying for Eastern was tough to recover from. He had status and a long career that he loved every day he flew planes. He did not want to go to another airline where he would have to take a demotion from captain, take a big cut in pay, and begin all over. In his inimitable way, he took a couple of jobs as a corporate executive and then decided that he needed a change in his life and he retired to contemplate what he would do. He was not ready to quit working.

It was about that time that I met Sandy who was living in the Orlando, Florida, suburbs. I was a widow of a couple of years who was becoming more active in multi-sports athletics with my triathlon club, the St. Pete Mad Dogs, and had recently finished my second triathlon. Sandy was telling me about all of his athletic adventures which included, but were not limited to: skydiving 600+ jumps plus one out of a 727 aircraft, karate, golf, fishing, track, sailing, scuba diving, riding a motorcycle on long trips, and running. He ran as a competitive masters runner for the Shore AC in New Jersey, preferring to run the mile but he performed his best at five-to-ten kilometers.

We have a lot in common in that we are contemporaries in age with only one year and 25 days between us. However, after a few dates, I discovered that he had no interest in doing anything athletic except lifting weights in his in-home gym. Plantar fasciitis prevented him from spending too much time on his feet. His day consisted most of the day trading stocks on his computer, playing poker online, and lifting weights. Not the outdoors man we talked about.

Soon the unbreakable link was established between the bicycle and the most dedicated rider I know. One day close to his 64th birthday, in March, 2004, I packed up a second bicycle on my Chevy Suburban and headed to Sandy's house for our once a week date. I was taking him on a picnic and a bike ride which I knew he would love. He was very surprised but was game to get on an old Kabuki 10-speed and come out with me. He complained about the dirty chain that was skipping and the fact that it needed to be cleaned and oiled. However there was joy on his face from the moment he passed me going up hill and took off down the road to the trail.

Within days, he was contemplating how he would get a new, slicker bicycle, reading everything he could about the sport, buying Lance Armstrong and Chris Carmichael's books, and started tearing up the Internet with inquires about the sport. It made our relationship stronger and reinforced his need for athletics and being out doing something physical every day. It also ultimately cured his plantar fasciitis although we never figured out how that actually happened. It became his new joy in life—not to be missed for even a single day.

His habit of writing down every detail of his athletic events every day has produced notebooks of data that he has used as tools for his training. Many of the things that he has learned over the years are in this book for you to use to improve your cycling; i.e., heart rate monitoring, lactic acid threshold, endurance training and all of the other things that will make you a better athlete.

Once he found out about what competitions were available, he registered for several local Senior Games and knew all of the people he would potentially race against and their winning times. He used a Specialized™ road bike to race in Port Charlotte, Florida, on March 19, 2005 and The Good Life Games in St. Petersburg, Florida, March 20, 2005 where, after being defeated by a national champion cyclist in his age group, he set his sights on never losing again. On May 5, he went under the 5K State of Florida record and topped the time of all of the 100 or so competitors in the 10K at The Villages, Florida, wearing his new, and now famous Zebra suit and riding his beautiful Guru custom-made time trial bike, fondly named, "Jezebel."

In sports and all endeavors, he prides himself on achieving perfection and his success has been accomplished through the desire to set goals, train hard, exceed expectations of his competitors, and win—just what and how to do it is what is in this book. His self-determination, will power, physical strength, and focus developed and it is what enabled him to put his injury aside and get back on the road to winning gold in his short career of cycling.

Sandy returned to competition at the Ormond Beach Senior Games, one year after his fracture, and seven months after shedding his neck brace. He won the time trial and defeated the defending state champion. One week later, he won both time trials at the Venice Senior Games.

The day that he dreamed about finally arrived on December 5, 2006—the Florida State Championships. He won the 5K time trial defeating the defending state champion and second-place finisher at the nationals by 14 seconds. Sandy's training and racing comeback and goals were accomplished and his dreams came true. "It was such an incredibly emotional experience after what I had been through the past year that, as I warmed down on my bike, tears were streaming down my face."

Two days later, he won the 20K road race on a break-away, finishing the race 20 seconds ahead of the peloton that included two defending state champions. It turned out to be the fastest time of the day—not only faster than the younger age groups, but also the second fastest time ever recorded for the 20K road race in the history of the Florida Senior Games competitions!

In June, 2007, he entered his first two United States Cycling Federation (USCF) events: The state road race and state time trial championships. He won the race on a break away and beat the second place finisher in the 20K time trial by 1:39, going under the state record by over two (2) minutes! The records below tell all.

State Championships Won After the Broken Neck:
December: 2006 to Present:

- Five (5) State of Florida, Senior Games, state time trial championships.
- One (1) State of Florida, Senior Games, state road racing championship.
- Three (3) United States Cycling Federation, State of Florida time trial championships.
- Two (2) United States Cycling Federation, State of Florida road race championships.

Records Held:
- Florida State Record -- 5 kilometer time trial, 65+ age group
- Florida state record -- 10 kilometer time trial, 65+ age group
- Cycled the fastest 20 kilometer time trial ever recorded in the USCF state time trial championships for someone over 65

Winner of the 2007 "AMS Masters Comeback Athlete" of the Year Award, *Masters Athlete Magazine*

To have had several excellent races at the beginning of his racing career and then being told to not even get on a bicycle was heartbreaking for someone of his boundless energy. We hope that this book will raise awareness of this upper cervical spinal injury and the need to wear a helmet. It will also demonstrate the possibility of coming back from such a catastrophic accident.

Our experiences at the onset of the injury demonstrated the need to go by your gut feeling and get second, third or more opinions when you know something is just not right and you are not getting the answer you want to hear. There is nothing wrong with questioning an outcome—just in not pursuing your doubts. If you leave a physician's office with doubts and questions, it is time to move on to another doctor and another possible solution.

Our quest to find a local cervical vertebrae specialist was akin to the Lewis G. Carroll great nonsense epic, *The Hunting of the Snark*. At times, it seemed hopeless as Sandy and I plowed through the vast resource of the Internet trying to find someone or someplace where we could find an answer as to whether or not his neck would heal. No one really knew—not even the best-of-the-best orthopedic surgeons.

We are on the roads of St. Petersburg and Pinellas County every day of the week or riding the Pinellas Trail that runs from St. Petersburg to Tarpon Springs. We see many things that make you want to scream, "Hey, you can break your neck if your dog on his leash crosses in front of your or my bike!" or "Announce when you are passing!" or "The law is three (3) feet for passing me!", and, the ultimate, "Take your earphones out!"

This book is a practical, easily-read and understood guide for all masters athletes—particularly those who desire to compete in races—spelling out everything from buying your bike, setting and achieving goals, training, bike maintenance, nutrition and health issues, and, ultimately, racing and winning gold medals. And there are a lot of tips to help every one of us ride, race, or work on our bikes more efficiently and economically.

The training and racing parts of the book are not in depth, complicated coaching, but a "how to" enjoy your cycling and provide you with basic, practical, and proven ways in which a masters athlete can work toward winning races. Sandy is a proponent of the "KISS" method of training—not the often over-complicated and sometimes difficult-to-follow methods we read about in many books. We hope that you will enjoy the journey Sandy took and be encouraged to get out and put in the time on your bike and then share the success story with your family and friends. If you can benefit from his experiences and his training, you can be a contender for the gold medals.

No one else can provide us the grit and determination to be a "success" in life--and that is measured by many different standards. However, there are many people who are instrumental in helping you achieve your goals and dreams from your grandparents, educators, and co-workers to your children. Sandy did not have mentors, but he set his expectations of himself high and used his intellect to approach each challenge with his prodigious intelligence and innate abilities.

Advice and good counsel make great companions on our journey through life. Sandy Scott's experience and words of wisdom on so many topics related to not only bicycle riding and racing but athletics in general have been circulating on the Internet for the past few years. There is hardly a person who has not heard the story of how he survived his injury and succeeded in coming back to bicycle racing, setting records, and winning all of the gold medals who is not in awe of his accomplishments.

This story of success built on a platform of a lifetime of experiences applies to many people who have overcome adversity and gone on to succeed in life. Each of us has it in us to excel and give 100% of our efforts to accomplish goals to meet our dreams. We hope that this story will inspire you and that the lessons on cycling will give you what you need to be a successful masters cyclist.

 # CHAPTER 1...

THE STORY BEGINS

Sandy's saga begins on the streets of Top of The World, Ocala, Florida. It was the fourth event of his bicycle racing career--part of the State of Florida Senior Games--and was a qualifier for the State of Florida Championship games. Senior Games are sponsored by each of the individual United States under the auspices of the National Senior Games Association.

The Florida races are held throughout the year in different venues around the state and the top five finishers in each age group qualify to compete for the State of Florida championships during the first week of December. The top two finishers of the state meet then go on to compete for Florida in the Senior Olympics held every two years as the National Championships for Senior Games. Sandy was qualified for the 2005 Florida State Championships and had set a goal of winning gold medals and breaking records in all his events.

We had driven to Top of The World on Saturday, October 22, checked into our hotel, and then took a drive to the course where Sandy would race two time trials the next day. We drove the course noting the holes in the road, bad curves, and hills that he would be navigating.

The weather was very windy and wet and it was a very difficult and technical course. There was no one in the recreation center on-site where the race was to begin and end so we went down to the sales office to find someone who could help us. A woman there told us that she thought the race had been cancelled due to the bad weather. This was not good news since Sandy had been in touch with the organizers previous to our traveling to Ocala and there was no indication that the race would not be held as planned.

After several hours, we did manage to get a contact via cell phone who informed us that the race was, indeed, not going to be held on that Sunday but would be postponed until the following weekend, October 30. To say that Sandy was disappointed was an understatement. Being a very organized and driven athlete in his quest for the gold medals, putting a crimp in the schedule is like driving a stake through his heart! Also, getting everything into the car, arranging pet sitters to take care of the two cats and two dogs, and book accommodations takes a lot of time, money, and planning well in advance of the event.

We spent the night near the race venue and he was 90% sure he did not want to do the race the next weekend. It was just an indication of the lack of management of the event and he was concerned about how safe it would be given what we had seen as lack of control on that very technical course—lots of twists and turns and an up-hill turnaround. After all, he had worked so hard to get his performance peaked and then, to have to come off of the high-ready state and back off, was too much stress.

But the thrill of the chase for the record times was too great and we did drive back to Top of The World for the October 30th race.

It was cold, sunny and an extremely windy day that Sunday, October 30, which raised a lot of concerns with Sandy because of his aerodynamic bicycle, fondly named "Jezebel"—a red and black beauty with yellow and red flames—custom-made for Sandy by Guru Manufacturing, Inc.™ of Montreal, Canada. The geometry of the bike and the Zipp™ rear disk wheel and 80mm front wheel equipped with a skinny 19mm tire pumped up to 150 psi for high speed, straight-line performance was a lot of bike to handle for anyone, not the least a novice bicycle racer.

Time trial bikes are meant to go straight and fast for the distance. The time trial racer is mentally prepared to put everything on the line and hopes that the course is true in length and straight out and back. Time trials are not like road racing: A chess game on wheels with a mass start and strategy developing within the peloton—an organized group of riders who take turns pulling the group at varying rates of speed as the race progresses. Then, there is a wild sprint at the end where the rider who has had the best (easiest) ride and conserved his or her effort "wheel sucking" often wins the race.

Time trial racing, known as "the race of truth," pits the racer against the clock with drafting off of other riders prohibited. It is every man or woman for him or herself; no whining at the end; no wheel sucking in the middle. Just courage and guts with no place to hide. The racer must be focused and have unwavering concentration, always seeing if the speed is fast enough, if he or she is riding the right place on the road, and thinking about making the turn for home at just the right speed so as not to lose precious seconds by coming out of clips or cutting it too wide.

The Top of The World course, called a "technical course" in the parlance of bicycle racing, was set up to go up and down hills and around sharp corners and had a turnaround at the top of the hill where the volunteer officials were stationed at the start/finish line. The ideal course is straight out and back with one, 180 degree turn at the half-way point.

Spectators were willy-nilly on either side of the race course, and one woman with several children including a toddler was on the side of the road leading up to the turnaround and just about 10 feet from it. There were not many spectators, but there were a lot of officials. Since this was my third race with Sandy as his "domestic," I tried to help the volunteers get organized and prepared as Sandy warmed up on the course. There were many questions as to how they should start and where the timers should be and who was doing what. I have been in races where the organizers ask family and friends there to support racers to act as "officials"—people who should know something about bicycle racing. That was the way it was at Top of The World.

The 5K time trial was about to begin and they were still trying to figure out what they had to do. This was not a good sign of control to me but I had to hold my tongue so as not to create a conflict just at race time.

The race began with the competitors being started at 30-second intervals. I knew that Sandy was intent on going 30 miles per hour on parts of the race and his concern about making turns at high speeds on Jezebel had me worried about all of the folks at the finish line. It is exciting in a time trial when you see someone coming to the finish line: muscles bulging and veins popping out, mouth open trying to fill their burned-out lungs with air, and, at least with Sandy, the retching after finishing having given it everything in his body for the win!

I tried to keep the spectators and the officials off of the road because, between them, it was chaotic at the finish line. When I saw Sandy coming up the hill to the turn, I began yelling, "Rider up" meaning he was coming in—and he was racing very fast. His tires were smoking! He looked great! He conquered the course! He won the first race!

When he realized he had won, he made a decision that he did not want to do the 10K.

He was very concerned by the number of turns, that it was held in a residential community with lots of drivers on the road, and the last three-quarters of a mile were uphill to the finish line. He had some other excuses: His stomach was upset; he had given it everything he had and felt there was no more to give; and his goal was to win the 5K with a great time and he did. During the 5K race he had maintained an average heart rate of 168 beats per minute with a peak of 176. For a

65 year old, 155 would have been his theoretical heart rate maximum.

My thought was that he just needed to get some food in him since he goes off to a race with a breakfast bar, glass of juice, and banana a couple of hours before. I told him to take some Clif Gel™ which is used to infuse a body with high carbohydrates before or during races. He did and felt much better and decided he would race. When Sandy went off of the line, he was feeling really strong and ready to win a second gold. I was happy that I would not have to hear him whine about not doing the second race. Little did I know…?

I must interject here that Sandy is the picture of a healthy, youthful male at 69 years old. He has lots of muscles from weight lifting, running, and bicycle riding. He is tall and slender and has excellent posture. He has four percent (4%) body fat—which I am always envious of— and he will ration his sweets so that he only eats one candy bar and a few cookies and a bowl of ice cream per day. You'll hear more about this "winner's diet" later in the book. He is very much disciplined— especially when getting ready to race!

The race was underway and it was close to seven minutes when Sandy should have been coming around. Other earlier starters were coming up and I was yelling, "racer up – get off of the course!" so that the toddler and officials would get off of the road. It made me very nervous to see them in the middle of the road because if they were hit, the rider would be in real jeopardy; he and the official could be badly hurt, and the toddler could be killed if hit!

Sandy was coming up the hill and I was yelling and, as he approached the corner for his turn, an official ran in front of him to the center of the course.

Sandy came around the turn; I was on his right as he cornered; I yelled out his time and said, "You are winning this!" The next thing I saw was his front wheel completely turned and perpendicular to the rear disk wheel Sandy out of his pedals and flying over his handle bars. It happened so fast and was so terrifying to see him as he speared the ground with his head. My thought was, "there goes number 2 …" I was running to him as he started to roll over onto his back. He was alive and he could move his arms and legs!

CHAPTER 2...

THE JOURNEY COMMENCES

He rolled over onto his back. "Where am I?" He asked. I told him very quietly that we were in Ocala at a time trial race. "A race, he asked?" "What race?" "Take it easy," I said and took off his helmet and proceeded to wipe the blood off of his face. "Where am I, Rosie?" He asked again." "You've had a bad accident, Sandy, and you need to take it easy because help is on the way." "What happened, Rosie?" "You did not complete the turn. Your front wheel was turned all the way to the left. The wind may have picked it up and you flew over your handlebars and speared the ground with your head. I thought you were dead, darling. "Just stay still." I was, of course, ecstatic that he knew my name and who I was. (As a note, I suffered a severe concussion with a fractured scull and had amnesia for a couple of days when I was 21. I did not know my name nor recognize friends who took me to the hospital). "The ambulance is on the way. You're going to be O.K..."

His helmet's visor had cut into his nose and there was a lot of blood on his face. Without really thinking, I took off his helmet and put my sweater under his head. That was a very bad thing to do for someone with a potentially broken neck or severe cervical vertebrae injury. Some of the spectators had come over to see if they could do anything. One of them was a doctor and he stayed close by. The race continued and the emergency vehicle came after what seemed like an eternity but was approximately 25 minutes.

The movies we see always have the loved one jumping into the back of the emergency vehicle with the victim and accompanying them to the hospital. This is not what happens—and it had happened to me before with my husband. He was swimming with our triathlon club, The St. Pete Mad Dogs, at his weekly Tuesday night swim at the Northshore Pool in St. Petersburg, FL. He was getting ready for a triathlon. He was healthy and took good care of himself. He died of Sudden Cardiac Arrest (SCA) when a blood clot in a minor artery seized up his heart. The EMT did not get there in time to shock his heart into beating. By the time I arrived at the pool, he was unresponsive. When they put him into the ambulance, I was not allowed to go with him.

And there I was with Sandy. We had only a little over a year together. There is nothing more traumatic than seeing someone you love in a position of total helplessness. When I saw Sandy hit the ground, all I could think of was brain trauma, inability to breath, quadriplegic, or brain dead. "There goes #2" was the immediate thought. How could he survive such an accident?

When he flipped over, my heart leaped. That was my tough guy with all of the muscles and thick head! I was sure that he would be OK. He could move his legs and arms; talk—although he was very confused—and he seemed to recognize me and our relationship. The ambulance arrived and they immobilized him on a palette and told me to follow them.

Little did I know that the hospital they were taking him to was almost one hour away. It was THE longest trip I have ever taken. I cannot tell you how my heart was pounding and the thoughts going through my mind about how he was doing in the ambulance and why was I not in there with him. I called my son, Ian, and told him what had happened. He gave me comfort in that Sandy could talk, breath, and move his arms and legs. From a professional athlete who has seen a lot of injuries to cyclists and had them himself, I got some comfort and the word to, "Calm down, Mom, he will be OK."

CHAPTER 3...

THE HOSPITAL EMERGENCY ROOM

"I was somehow aware of the fact that I was in an ambulance, but I had no idea why I was there. There was an attendant at my side and I asked, "Why am I here?" He stated that I had been injured in a cycling accident while participating in a race at the Top of the World (a community in Ocala, FL). I told him that I had not participated in a bicycle race that day, and that I had never heard of the place. I remember trying to get my brain to remember the incident, but I could recall nothing."

"My body was in such deep shock that I was not aware of the acute pain until we arrived at the hospital. I have no recollection of being taken to an examination room, but I remember being in one and experiencing intense pain in my head such that I had never had before."

"Rosie was there with me asking when we would see a doctor and would they take care of cleaning up my hands and face that was really a bloody mess. The pain was heightened considerably when I was taken to radiology for x-rays. I recall the technician requesting that I flex and extend my neck in ways that caused me considerable pain, but he assured me that those positions were necessary to accurately assess my injuries."

"When they returned me to the ER, my stretcher was put in the hallway and a nurse came and said that they would be administering morphine through an IV that would take care of the pain. I was looking forward to the relief and was surprised when it started and I felt that nice warm feeling of it coursing through my veins—that was all. My head did not stop screaming at me that it really hurt! I still felt very confused. I had never been admitted to a hospital and had no idea of what to expect for treatment. I just knew that there was a big problem when the morphine did not do its job of stopping the pain."

I was concerned for Sandy because I have seen first hand what happens when they do not catch a hematoma of the brain immediately. He wasn't dead yet, but he could have a stroke or have irreparable damage to his prodigious brain from hemorrhaging. We had been there for a few hours and we had still not had a doctor's attention.

After another hour or so, the nurse came by and conveyed the radiologist's review of the brain scan as being "a severe neck strain" and that was all. I could not believe it and did not really want Sandy to leave the hospital area.

Sandy was released from the hospital without ever seeing a doctor and told to put hot and cold compresses on his neck and see an orthopedic specialist the following week. We took the x-Rays with us. The next most incredible thing after not seeing a doctor was that he was allowed to walk out of the hospital unassisted after having had a morphine drip for at least an hour. Having had many trips to the hospital and day surgery, I know that they were remiss in allowing that. Even for minor surgery, they always put you in a wheel chair and take you out to the curb and have your ride there and you in it before they leave.

If only they had taken us to a hospital with a trauma center. There is a whole set of protocols at a trauma center and doctors trained in their use that insures that anyone with an injury such as Sandy's would have been scanned immediately. However, we had no choice in the decision of where the ambulance took us.

"I recall that the pain was unbearable. Rosie got me into the SUV and we proceeded to my home in Lake Mary. Every bump and turn in the road caused me to flinch with the excruciating pain. I have a high tolerance of pain and sometimes don't even take pain-deadening drugs even when I have teeth drilled!"

We got home, started Sandy on the compresses and aspirin, and I called a friend in NJ who is an excellent spinal surgeon. Jim Cole said that we should get to the orthopedist ASAP. It was Sunday, so I waited until Monday and called my doctor in St. Petersburg. They could not fit us in for over six weeks. Hard to believe!

"Although I had virtually no neck movement, and was suffering rather severe pain I knew that I had to find a way to not lose my conditioning. The state championship cycling races were in 5 weeks, and I intended to not only be there – I intended to win!"

"Three days after the accident, I commenced riding my bicycle on an indoor trainer. I rode 70 minutes daily, well under my usual training time. With no improvement to my neck mobility or lessening of the pain, I sought chiropractic help for my neck sprain. I was about to experience perhaps the most pain I have ever felt."

"Rosie called a chiropractor in St. Petersburg that would see me on Wednesday, 11/7/05, when we got back to her home which was seven days after the accident. I brought the X-rays of my head with me to the visit. The chiropractor I was supposed to see was not there, but they did start me on electronic stimulation and massage. The next day, I saw the chiropractic doctor I had been highly recommended to for diagnosis."

"The doctor examined me, and, at one point as he stood to my rear, he held my head in his hands, told me to relax, and suddenly twisted my neck. I let out a scream which must have been heard two blocks away. I was in so much pain and in such a hurry to get out of that torture chamber that I did not remember a word he said. I left the office with considerably more pain than I arrived with and a deep concern as to my medical problem."

On 11/10, two days later, we had an appointment with a board-certified spinal surgeon after I made a frantic call to the orthopedic practice where I have had surgery and I practically begged them to take Sandy because of his pain. This was approximately nine (9) days after the accident.

The surgeon looked at the X-rays and decided that they were so badly done that he could not use them to diagnose the problem. He was amazed that we had not seen a doctor. He kept the x-Rays and made an appointment at a radiology center for Sandy to have a CT scan and MRI of the cervical vertebra on November 11.

"The CT scan was administered and the technician told me she was going to review the films. A few minutes later she returned to my side as I lay still in the CT scan machine. She said, 'Mr. Scott, don't move, I need to get the doctor.' Very soon thereafter, a physician appeared with the technician and said, 'I don't want to scare you Mr. Scott, but you have a broken C1 cervical vertebra. Your neck is broken.' I had mixed feelings immediately: First, I was somewhat pleased that someone had found the source of the pain; then, my immediate thought was that I was never going to race again."

"To say the least, that was a rather startling revelation, and I thought back to the chiropractor violently twisting my neck. The potential consequences of that were rather frightening to ponder. They would not let me move until they gingerly handled my neck and head and fitted me with a very stiff neck brace. They called the doctor and an appointment was set up with the spinal surgeon on 11/14 for a consult and discussion about what could be done." It was truly the most frightening and depressing day of my life to know that I could be dead with just a fall or something hitting me in the head."

CHAPTER 4...

DISCOVERY

On November 14th, in Sandy's visit with the orthopedic surgeon, we discovered that he had been quite fortunate in that a C1 fracture--the rarest of all neck fractures--is immediately fatal in about 50 percent of the cases with many residual deaths typically occurring over the next few days after the accident.

"I was now painfully aware of the fact that I would not be competing in the state championships, and perhaps I would never compete again. The doctor was not optimistic for this type of fracture to heal in a young person no less a 65 year old. He decided to take a wait-and-see line of treatment and advised that I would have another scan in one month."

"I continued to ride my trainer in my garage for 70 minutes daily wearing my brace, not being able to move my neck, and having rather intense pain as my constant companion. Riding a trainer is one of the hardest exercises I have ever done. It is nothing like being on the road for 50 miles. Every minute is painful and, without the ability to turn my head, there was no relief in moving about on the saddle."

"Quite stupidly, I commenced training with weights three weeks after the fracture. We have a gym in our home so I did not have to go outside of my safe zone. I was getting perpetually yelled at by Rosie who thought this was a very stupid thing to do. My thought was that the doctor did not say I could not do it. When someone is as driven as I am to stay fit, the only option is to push on with what you do normally. Weight lifting was a three-time per week workout and it was going to get done."

"The one concession I made was using lesser weights. For example, my warm-up weight for doing bench presses is 135, and then I progress up in weight with each set. I simply did all of my sets with 135 pounds. I would lie there pressing 135 pounds over my head hoping I would not suddenly hear a 'cracking' sound."

That routine of Sandy pushing himself and me yelling at him to not be so thick headed continued for a seemingly-never-ending five (5) months.

"Pain was my constant companion, but I refused to give up my conditioning. I was already thinking about the state championships of the following year. I cannot describe to you how lost I felt without the physical exercise and driven-schedule I had been on to make my first State of Florida championship games."

 # CHAPTER 5...

RESOLUTION AND REBELLION
THE YING AND YANG OF A TRUE MASTER ATHLETE

If I were to tell you that the five months of going back for more scans was more painful than the pain in the neck Sandy was suffering, you would probably not believe me. However, it was the ultimate tease: See the doctor; have the scan done; see the doctor; have him tell us that there was no improvement.

At the end of five months, the doctor told Sandy that he would have to see a neurosurgeon about having his cervical vertebrae fused and pins put in his skull so that he could walk around without having an accidental hit to his head that would kill him. We both looked upon this with skepticism and, with the thought of one last, great push on the Internet, we left the orthopedist's office resolved to finding a better doctor and way to proceed.

The solution to have his vertebrae fused meant that he would not be able to ever ride or race his bicycle. His entire life would be changed from being an extremely strong and persistent athlete to a couch potato—if he survived the surgery! In his heart, the rebellion to not give up began.

If you were to look at the inside of your head, you would see that the C-1 is the vertebra that the spinal cord travels through (See Illustrations). It is also way up in your head and, therefore, as I said earlier, if it gets broken, it usually kills you or puts you on life support because breathing normally is interfered with. Many die because they stop breathing before artificial breathing assistance can be implemented. If you survive the break and get on breathing support, you will never get disconnected from it.

In addition, there have been very few operations where the outcome of this procedure was successful. A patient is just as likely to get killed on the operating table as he or she is likely to be killed from the accident. There just are not enough people who have survived the surgery to tell about it.

The search for the snark was on again. The troops were on the march—Sandy and me. Over the Internet, Sandy was able to find a spinal surgeon at the University of Pennsylvania who was very well known for having operated on the upper cervical vertebrae and had a minimally invasive procedure that was not as limiting as having a spinal fusion.

"I called the surgeon at the University of Pennsylvania and spoke to him at length about my broken neck. I had all of my scans and the result from my last MRI on CD and asked if he could take a look at them to see if there was a chance that he could help me. He said he would and I sent them to him express mail."

"Just so you know, I always wanted to be a physician and am excellent at digging deep and finding out all of the facts for anything that affects me, my family, or my friends. When asked to help, there is no limit to what I can find out about almost anything on the Internet. To say that I went into my CT scans and MRIs and learned everything there was to know about my fracture—it was a frontal break—and who had done what in the medical field for this type of injury would be an understatement. There was so little information available, it was pathetic and almost everything pointed to the fact that I could be dead quicker than I could be healed of this break."

"I waited for a few days to give the doctor time to evaluate the information and then called when a reasonable amount of time had passed. When he finally returned my calls, he said that he was returning the disk because he was unable to read it… This was disappointing in that he is supposed to be a leader in the field. I was so depressed by that thought, but he did salvage my faith in the medical profession by referring me to a doctor at the University of Miami who he considered the "expert of experts" in cervical vertebrae surgery."

Sandy was so down and did not want to proceed further. He was ready to just give up and call a neurosurgeon. After persuading him that we should at least go to Miami, he asked me to call Dr. Eismont which I did.

When you have a very famous doctor who is a specialist in such a rare injury, your chances of getting to talk to him are almost nil without a reference from another colleague in the field. I called and spoke to his office, described Sandy's injury, told them about the doctor in St. Petersburg and that the doctor in Pennsylvania was referring us to him as the very best, and asked if I could make an appointment for Sandy. They said that we could make an appointment to see Dr. Eismont, but his first opening was in August. I could not believe it! It was only February! I did not know if I could keep Sandy going until then. I said that I would call back.

"I could not believe that I would have to be in the neck brace until August. It was a blow to my entire being. You cannot imagine what it is like to sleep on your back every night, eat, shower, and live your life in a neck brace. On top of that, I was still doing my 70 minutes per day on my bike trainer in my garage. I was really ready to give up and have the surgery because the life I was leading was totally not me."

When we could not see Dr. Eismont until August, I called my dear friend and orthopedic surgeon for a second time. I told Dr. Jim Cole what had been going on with the surgeons and asked Jim if he could recommend someone at The Hospital for Special Surgery in New York City who could look at the scans. It is a great hospital and Jim had done a residency there.

He made some inquiries and called us back and talked to us about the #1 guy in all of New York City who would look at the scans for some ridiculous amount of money but there was no guaranty that he would actually work with Sandy. We thought about it and then asked Jim to get back to him and tell him we were interested in seeing someone as soon as possible. Sandy did not need a doctor to tell him what he could see on the scan. He wanted a decisive solution from the surgeon.

Having been not only an executive secretary in my first career and a sales executive in one of my longest careers, I was not about to just give up on my target—Dr. Eismont. I called the office back and spoke to the very friendly and concerned woman who had helped me on the first call. I told her the status again and asked her if there were any doctors in the Tampa Bay area who studied on fellowships under Dr. Eismont. Yes, indeed, there were two within a short distance of our home! BINGO!

 # CHAPTER 6...

DO YOU BELIEVE IN MIRACLES?

When one reaches the limits of pain and suffering, it is easy to cling to any thread that offers hope. Sandy was at the point where, in his mind, he did not have a thread to hold onto. When I told Sandy that we had two excellent, local doctors who had worked on fellowships under Dr. Eismont to call for appointments, he was as excited as he could be at the time. It was now mid-March and our last appoint with the orthopedic surgeon in St. Petersburg was February 2.

Sandy did a lot of research on the two physicians and was really impressed with both of their credentials. However, he was drawn to Dr. Marc Weinstein for his interest in sports. Not only did he appear to be an excellent physician, he also had been a collegiate athlete. He rowed on the varsity crew team of Rutgers. This put him in the prime spot for review because Sandy's son, Evan, had been an outstanding varsity crew member at Syracuse. Having such an athlete for a physician would mean that he would have a strong understanding of the way Sandy thinks about his sport and regard for Sandy's desire to find another solution than spinal fusion. We decided we would call Dr. Weinstein after we got the last scan in St. Petersburg. The prospect of seeing Dr. Weinstein was exciting and depressing at the same time. At that time, I don't think Sandy believed that anything good could happen and he was in a real funk.

Some of our friends kept in close touch. Roger Burke, one of my St. Pete Mad Dog Triathlon Club buddies, called and visited and helped to keep his spirits up. Others were regular e-Mail contacts such as the president of the bike club, Wendy Menne, and Dr. Don Ardell.

At one point, we called Roger in an emergency to come and help us put together a couple of chairs we had bought. We were about to see flying parts all over our living room from the shear frustration Sandy was having in not being able to manipulate the furniture and get the screws into the holes that were in difficult places for a man who could not move his head!

Learning through research on the Internet, Sandy could basically tell a surgeon how he would perform the surgery. He was blessed with a prodigious brain that never stops thinking, "What if?" but his pain overcame his intellect on many days when it seemed so futile to think that he could be on his bike, riding like the wind downtown to beat up on all the "girls"—his name for the boys in the peloton who gave just a hint that they could not keep up!

"Rosie kept reminding me that I was alive and that was a miracle, and incessantly told me to stop whining and be happy that I could walk and talk and was not in a diaper. I don't know if I could have survived on my own without going nuts. My kids were in MD, VA, and TX and she was the only one I could really communicate my frustration to."

"I had a board-certified spinal surgeon pushing me to surgery that I did not believe would work and with no guarantee that I would be alive or able to live without life support when I got off of the operating table. I had never been sick and, therefore, never had an experience of being helpless and in the hands of other people. I am very self-sufficient to a fault and hate to even ask for help. I guess that is part of my airline pilot mentality."

"My surgeon basically said that, since it had not healed by then, five months, it was a non-union and would always be that way. He warned that I was in grave danger of going through life with the potential of dropping dead if I fell and hit my head or had just a minor mishap such as hitting my head on an obstruction."

"'There are two choices," he said, and then went on to describe them in a matter-of-fact way. The first potential way to take care of the non-union was that the neurosurgeon would fuse my C-1 to the occiput (the base of the skull); or, the second choice, where he would fuse C-1 to C-2. Either of those choices would render me with a permanent, minimum 50% of loss in neck mobility, and, hence end my cycling career—that is if he managed to do it at all."

"I cannot describe the pain to you that I had every minute of every day and night from October 30 to February 2. My normal eating, personal hygiene, exercise, and sleeping habits had to be changed to accommodate the wearing of the hard collar. I was forced to sleep on my back and had electrodes which were supposedly stimulating the production of the sticky stuff to fill in the gap in my C1 attached to me; taking a shower lost all of its pleasure—everything--where I went and everything I did was a constant reminder of the real 'pain in the neck'."

And then we called Dr. Marc Weinstein at The Center for Spinal Disorders at the Florida Orthopaedic Institute. After telling the receptionist that we had been recommended to him by Dr. Eismont, we were given an appointment for March 15. To say we were excited at the prospect of seeing this very talented and well-known spinal surgeon in such a short time is an understatement.

The final scan for the doctor in St. Petersburg was March 13th and Sandy took those to the appointment with Dr. Weinstein.

On March 15th, Dr. Weinstein reviewed Sandy's scans. They had a lot of discussion about the fact that he was well qualified to do the surgery on the C-1, but would not do it as he would be the only one to benefit—financially.

He felt that Sandy's C-1 break was very unusual in that the normal break of that vertebra is in two pieces somewhat like snapping a potato chip in two. He could not see anything that showed that there was matter developing in the break.

Dr. Weinstein said that it was so unusual that Sandy could be walking and talking for the past five months with this break that he asked if he would mind if he took his case and showed the scans at his weekly meeting at the University of South Florida, Tampa. The meeting was to be attended by orthopedic surgeons, neurosurgeons and radiologists.

"Of course, I said 'Yes' to Dr. Weinstein's request to use my case as a teaching tool at the university. He gave me such hope and confidence in his capabilities that anything he did that could potentially help me was welcomed. Also, he was just beginning to cycle and asked me all kinds of questions about training and what to buy! How could he not be terrific!"

"I was so elated that this fine doctor was telling me what I had felt all along that I did not need invasive surgery. As a matter of fact, I found that there were lots of complications from surgery in the area of the C-1 including very bad outcomes from having surgeons operating on this very hard-to-reach area at the base of the skull. The C-1 fracture is the rarest of all breaks. It is so rare a break that there few surgeons who can do it. In fact, many orthopedic surgeons and radiologists have never seen a C-1 fracture in their practices. Also, there are so many fatalities at the time of the break and so few surgeons have actually had the experience of working on C-1 fractures. In fact, the surgery is so delicate that the doctor in St. Petersburg said he was not qualified to do that type of operation and the neurosurgeon would probably not be experienced in C-1 specifically, he was simply well known for working in that part of the anatomy."

"I was given an appointment to have further scans taken for a review of different angles. Dr. Weinstein told me he would have had me out of the collar in two weeks but to keep the hard collar until he further reviewed the scans with the other doctors."

"On March 29, I had my second visit to Dr. Weinstein. He said that the scans show that the break is stable and that there was really nothing he would do at this point except to schedule further scans once each month. He was hoping that he would see some gelatinous filler begin to form because I was in such good shape. He recommended more calcium, less weight lifting overhead, physical therapy and massage to relieve the pain and the atrophied muscles and arthritis involved from the brace being on too long."

"Apparently one or two of the physicians in the group expressed skepticism that I had, indeed, suffered a C-1 fracture. They believed that the C-1 break was congenital. Otherwise, how could I exercise the way I was and why was there no healing after five months? There was still a 2mm gap in the anterior arch of my C-1 vertebra. Dr. Weinstein disagreed with that assessment, and that opinion later to be vindicated."

"Dr. Weinstein cautioned me that if I chose to go out on my bicycle, that I could die if I had a fall. I told him I would take my chances! Hard to believe! No guts, no glory! Yippee! I could hardly contain my glee! My life was back. I followed his few orders to a "T" and began physical therapy."

PHYSICAL THERAPY

"Dr Weinstein had recommended a physical therapist, but Rosie knew of a very special doctor of physical therapy, Dr. Diane Hartley, of Hartley Healthcare Services. She is very involved with the best TMJ (Temporomandibular Joint Syndrome) surgeon in the U.S. and has provided his post-operative patients with pain management and mobility therapy for many years. Rosie had a B&B and was the preferred lodging for Dr. Mark Piper's patients who were recuperating from surgery and needed a lot of TLC. She had also gone to Hartley Healthcare when she had a need post-surgery. She said, ' Dr. Hartley is the best!' and she was not wrong. I started on the second part of getting my neck well, and I was glad that I had such a great team of physicians to work with."

"Dr. Hartley was astonished that I was walking, talking, breathing, and riding my bike. She indicated that she was going to proceed very cautiously in that she had never given therapy to someone with a broken neck and had never personally seen a case of a broken C-1. She called in one of her interns and said that she would never ever see another case like mine and wanted her to be in on my therapy."

"After a few sessions, Dr. Hartley asked if she could present my case to a conference in Las Vegas to which I agreed. I had ten hours with Dr. Hartley, commencing on April 3rd."

"My next appointment with Dr. Weinstein was scheduled for the 26th of April. This was for observing any improvements in my ability to extend my neck in a couple of directions. He checked the extensions—pushing the neck upwards, and flexion—pushing my neck downwards--of my neck. At that point, he prescribed four more hours of physical therapy which continued until May 3."

"I returned to his office on July 26 where Dr. Weinstein took two more X-rays and that is when he even wavered a bit, showing me the arthritic involvement and thinking that the injury was going to be a non-union. He was not nuts about me running around and racing on my bike with a broken C-1 vertebra. This was for good cause. As a person with 657 skydives and 12 hours and 40 minutes of free-fall time, including jumping out of everything from a hot-air balloon to a jet airplane and over 15,000 hours as a commercial pilot, I am not the type to turn away from danger. In fact, I embrace it—actually, I need it!"

CHIROPRACTIC CARE

"I had completed my 14 hours of physical therapy and I was able to ride my road bike quite well. Unfortunately, I did not have sufficient neck mobility to ride my time trial bike. I could ride, as long as I didn't have to see where I was going! I simply could not lift my neck sufficiently to see down the road in the very aggressive position required to be sufficiently aerodynamic."

"One day I was riding home from a club ride, and I stopped at a red light where a fellow I did not know came from behind me on his bike and started up a conversation. He knew who I was and introduced himself to me as Dr. Ed Schroeder, a chiropractic physician who owned the Back Pain Relief Clinics in St. Petersburg. He had talked to Rosie during a St. Pete Mad Dog triathlon club training ride and heard that I had fractured my neck. He also heard about my bad experience with another chiropractor and was sorry about that. He told me that he could help me regain my neck mobility. I was quite skeptical, but I scheduled an appointment with his daughter, Dr. Rhonda Schroeder."

"I commenced twice a week treatments with Dr. Rhonda, as she likes to be called, in September of 2006. The treatments were comprised of electro-heat therapy, massage, and manipulation. The goal was to break up the scar tissue and deal with the arthritis that had formed around my upper cervical vertebrae."

"The treatment regimen was completely successful – I was able to properly ride my time trial bike within a few weeks and by early December, I won my first time trial state championship!"

After all of the therapy, we settled down to a new riding routine where Sandy would leave the house somewhere around 7:00 a.m. and return at about Noon with stories of all the road warriors and the sprints and near-misses incurred on the Pinellas Trail and on the road with the St. Pete Bike Club.

Sandy came home one day and told me about a horrific accident that had taken place. He could hardly believe his luck and so we will share it with you.

"I had two close calls when I commenced riding outdoors with my neck still broken. I still had a two (2) millimeter gap in the anterior arch of my C1 cervical vertebrae. The physician's warning that if I fell I could easily die was always in the back of my mind."

"One day I was traversing the Pinellas Trail in the St. Petersburg area. I was travelling along at about a 20 mph pace and I could see a large group of riders coming from the opposite direction. They were spread out across the complete trail, and as I got within a reasonable distance, I yelled to them to move over. No one moved and at the last moment, I had to swerve off the trail to avoid a rider going down the left edge of the trail. I hit some sand and my bike went down, and my head tapped the pavement at the edge of the trail. I exited that incident with some road rash after giving the riders a tutorial on proper use of the bicycle trail."

"Soon thereafter, I decided to join one of the faster groups on a Saturday morning group ride of the St. Pete Bike Club. It was a fast ride with the intent of maintaining at least 26 mph with many forays over 30 mph. We had just made a fast turn on to a narrow roadway and the group was in frenzy as if they were contesting the Tour de France. We were four abreast and travelling about 27 mph. I was thinking to myself, "What am I doing in this group with a broken neck?"

"Just then, a cyclist in front of me and to my left hit the rear wheel of the guy in front of him. A multiple bicycle accident occurred, and I can still remember a bicycle flying through the air heading towards me. I thought, "Oh no!" The bicycle hit me hard on the side of my left leg leaving me with a bloody gash, but I somehow managed to keep my bike upright. It was starting to seem that I was on a quest to kill myself on a bicycle."

To say that we were thankful that he did not suffer serious injury with the flying bicycle is an understatement. It was his fate. He was destined to survive and thrive on the mere fact that he was outdoors and riding every day of the week as if it were his last day on earth.

In the meantime, Dr. Weinstein did not expect that the C-1 would heal and it would be a non-union and thought that Sandy should seriously consider surgery instead of going through life with a broken neck. He scheduled one more scan for August 2, 2006.

"The last scan was the best. It must have been the prospect of having a spinal fusion and never celebrating the gold medals again that caused the non-union to heal. The good news was celebrated, and the next day I was into my training routine with more dedication than I had previously. It was like being re-born and I was on my way to win the State of Florida time trials and make the 2007 Senior National Games.

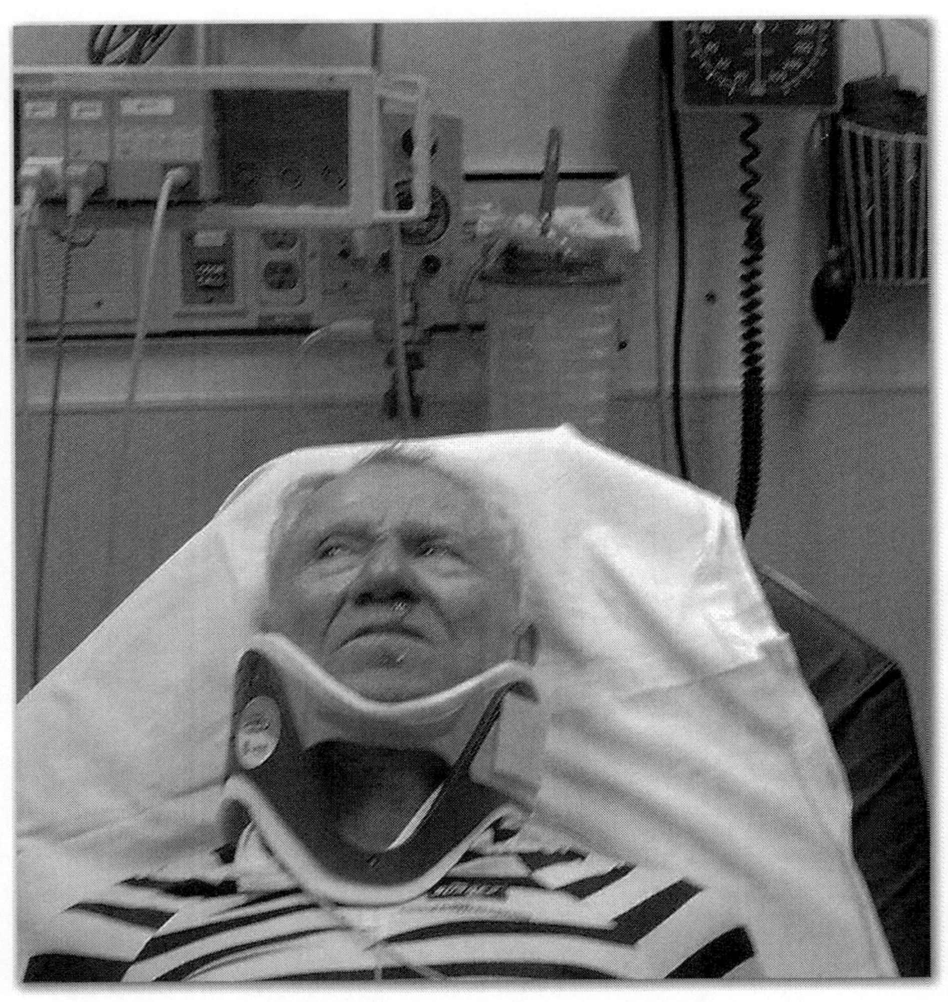

Sandy in Ocala Regional Hospital Emergency Room

Sandy showing off his first Florida State Champion jersey

On his way to winning the gold for the 10K TT, The Villages,
USGA, 2005

State USCF Championship Gold Medal Winner, 20K, 2009

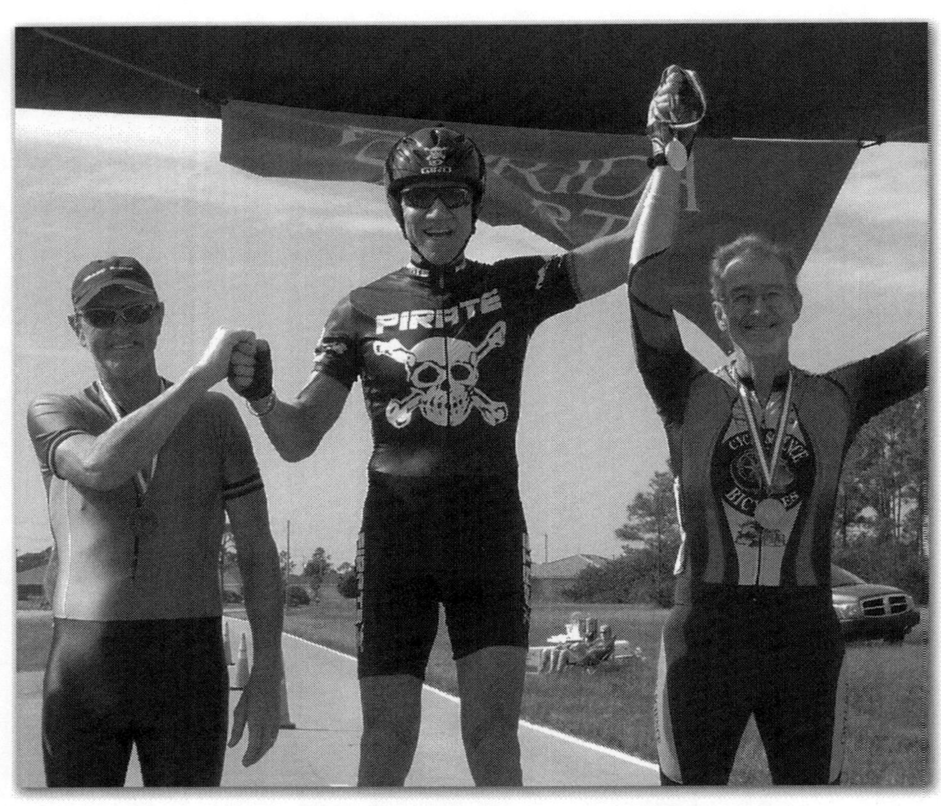

State of Florida 5K and 10K Champion, USGA, 2008

Rosie and Sandy'at his 6th career race—The second race after recovering from the broken neck—Venice, FL, 11/06

CHAPTER 7...

TRANSITIONS: TRAINER TO TRAINING

Getting Sandy off of the trainer and back on the road was bittersweet. Knowing that he had come so close to death and cheated it created a human machine the likes of which I had never seen. To say that he is a bit compulsive about training is putting it mildly. If I am not out on my bike every day or not doing some physical exercise, it is taken as an opportunity to point out to me that winners have no excuses for not training.

Since 2006 August when he got out of the garage and back on the road to training with goals in mind, he has missed just one day. He can tell you exactly when and why it was because of the detailed records he keeps.

Using a computer program, CycliStats™ and his Polar Heart Rate Monitor™ he can tell you and show you the details of each ride and race. I always kid him and call him "The Count" after the Sesame Street character that always has to add up the numbers.

Sandy will leave the house at approximately 6:30AM, on the days that he is going to go to downtown St. Pete and ride with our bike club. Since they do not leave the parking lot of the Northshore Pool until 8:30AM, he gets 15 miles warm-up ride to the venue and then will ride around until the ride begins; take the 20-40 mile ride to a beautiful, county park called Ft. DeSoto or go to Pass-a-Grille, return downtown, and then come home. This may be 55-80 miles. On one occasion, he returned with over 100 miles!

On those rides, usually Monday, Thursday, and Saturday, he will terrorize the group by always having to go faster. If he is feeling his breakfast bar and banana, he will come home somewhere around 12:00PM and tell me about how beat he is and how he went 33 miles per hour dropping people and pulling the remainder until he had only the Cat 1 and young riders on his wheel and his training partner, Jerry Rush—who is 30 years younger.

Now, you would think that a man of 69 who broke his neck would have a healthy respect for riding that fast in a pack. Well, he does! He does not ride in the pack. He always wants to be up front, staying out of trouble—causing it perhaps, but safe in his mind. When my son, Ian, the retired professional triathlete, recently came to visit, he took great joy in having him pull with him down to Ft. DeSoto dropping other riders like flies.

If, on the way home on the Pinellas Trail, he is passed by someone who he thinks is passing him because he thinks he is old and slow, he will put on the speed and pass him and then proceed to tear up the road getting out of his sight. His handle on Google mail is "PedalMasher" and I can tell you that it fits his personality to a "T".… This is the mentality of a true bicycle racer. It is like our rescued, retired racing greyhound, Kitty Hawke: If she sees a rabbit, she wants to chase it.

On Sandy's recovery days, he goes from being the "Road Warrior" to being "Mr. Laid Back." This happens on Tuesday, Friday, and Sunday. These are the days when I go out with Sandy and we do three (3) parks and the Pinellas Trail. We usually start in Millennium Park which is very close to our home. It is approximately 2.5 miles around. The warm-up is usually three turns around the park and then we leave it and head up to the Trail. If I am late in leaving the house and I get there when it is almost 9:00AM, I will find him and then offer to turn around and go out of the park. This is the wrong thing to do because he will tell me that I am sloughing off and really not interested in training. This embarrassment works, even though I would never tell him it does.

We head up the Trail at about 11-12 mph. This is so slow for me because this is really my training ride so I will do "Fartlek" riding which means I do intervals very fast when I have a long stretch of Trail and then slow down for a minute or so, then pick up my speed, and so forth.

Before the end of the ride—usually 2.5 hours—we will also go through Walsingham Park for at least a couple of turns; head back to the Trail; hit Taylor Park for a couple of turns, and then head up the Trail for a few more miles, and we return home when he has completed 35-36 miles. I have completed 32 miles if I can stand to be in the saddle that long, and he has done a turn around our neighborhood to complete his miles. It is called dedication and commitment—training to win.

"Consistency is everything. When I was a runner, I trained the same way. Whether it is raining or snowing, cold or hot, or you are not feeling quite right, you need to get out and do your workout. This morning was the first time in months that I had to set up the trainer in front of the TV and workout. It was raining all night and day—a rare occurrence here in Florida. Your competition will be training so you need to keep that in mind."

We are heading into the guts of the game we know as "training." Each of us has a particular way of working our bodies and minds so that, when we get to race day, we are prepared to meet the competition. For Sandy, it is consistency of training and dedication to his exercise no matter a broken neck or other malady. For many of us, training is doing a good workout at least five days a week with some time for fun and family and we look to our competition as friends we want to beat—not beat up!

Each of us has it in us to get out on race day and do our best or we would not be there. With Sandy's training methods, I have achieved some new goals and have put new effort into my training—especially doing intervals in preparation for the USCF Florida Championships— in which I won my age group in the 20K time trial, and 2009 Senior

Olympics, where I set a personal best in the 5K time trial. His method works and it is easy to understand:

Consistency in Training + Miles + Dedication = Winning.

CHAPTER 8...

COMPETITIVE CYCLING

Prior to dealing with the specifics of training and racing for the master athlete, we will cover the subject of competitive cycling in general.

Many of you are probably active competitors, but for those who have not experienced the exciting world of cycling competition, let me give you an overview of what is available for the masters competitor.

Primarily, we will be speaking of road events, but understand there are many track, off road, and ultra-cycling events available throughout the United States and world—something for everyone who has it in them to want to put everything in their heart and mind into their sport.

Most states have Senior Games competitions throughout the year to qualify for the state championship events. Various sports are offered including cycling. Here in Florida, for example, the Senior Games comes under the auspices of the Florida Sports Foundation. You can find a schedule of all local qualifying events and information about the state championships on its website: www.flasports.com. The National Senior Games Association oversees the events nationally and organizes and runs the Senior Olympics every two years. Its website is www.nsga.com.

In most states, you must qualify for the state championships by placing at least fifth in your five-year age group in a local event for the sport in which you wish to participate. To qualify for the Senior Olympics, The Summer National Games, the competitors must place at least second at a state championship event to qualify.

The cycling events offered in the Senior Games system are the 5K & 10K time trial events, and the 20K and 40K road race events.

There are also various cycling events offered under the auspices of the USCF (United States Cycling Federation), including state and national championship events. Unlike the Senior Games, which offers competition in five-year age groups commencing with age 50, the USCF has a full array of age group and classification (various categories) competitions. In the local USCF events, the master events are categorized in the following groups: Masters 35+, Masters 45+ and Masters 55+. In the state and national championship events, however, the USCF reverts to five-year age groups. Unlike the Senior Games, there is no need to qualify to compete in the state and national USCF championships. Your racing age is the age that you will attain by December 31st of the year of the race. One exception is the Senior Olympics at which your racing age is your actual age on the day of the competition.

To compete in USCF events, one must purchase an annual license ($60). More information on its events can be found on its website at www.usacycling.org. The USCF State Championships awards winners—who must be state residents—a "State Champion" jerseys. The U.S. National Championships awards the winners "Stars and Stripes" jerseys—both are very special as are the winners.

Those of you who are interested in World Championship competition, the UCI World Cycling Championships are held every August in Austria. Although the following website is written in German, the results are in English so you can compare your times with past performances at the event. Check out the website: www.masterswm.org/v4/?start/en

Domestically, the Huntsman World Senior Games are held in Utah every October. It is an incredibly well run event and offers cycling competitions in various cycling disciplines including time trials, road races, criteriums, and mountain bike events. If you compete in the "open" class, you can win a legitimate, "rainbow" world champion jersey at these events. They also offer events for novice riders apart from the open class. Both of the above venues offer competition in five-year age groups. Please visit its site at: http://www.seniorgames.net Here in St. Petersburg, monthly time trials are held on the first Tuesday and Thursday of the month. The races are sponsored by local bicycle shops and the charge to participate is somewhere in the range of $10-$15/race. The races are usually 15K or 20K and are held after 6:00 PM so, for those who work, it is a great opportunity to get out and race your heart out once a month. This gives you great experience for bigger events. Prizes for overall and age-group winners are awarded at the end of the series. Check with your local bicycle shops to see if they do this. If not, perhaps you can get them interested. It is wonderful for marketing their shops.

TIME TRIAL RACING EQUIPMENT
THE MIT CENTER FOR SPORTS INNOVATION STUDY

Start your engines! Let's talk about equipment for competing in cycling events—and, in particular, time trial races. Making the investment in proper clothing, accessories, and your bicycles for racing before you start training will give you an excellent chance to develop your skills right from the beginning.

If you have never participated in a Senior Games cycling event, you will be surprised to know that it is very competitive with very serious, talented, and dedicated athletes. Here in Florida, for example, I have had the pleasure of competing against four (4) national and two (2) world champions in my five-year age group races. I have competed in events with five (5) Olympic cyclists. Unless you have the genetics of Lance Armstrong (and perhaps even then), at the minimum, you will need the proper equipment to be competitive in a cycling time trial event.

Understanding how performance is affected by aerodynamics is extremely important to the serious bicycle racer who wants to win the gold medals. There were some surprising findings revealed through a study conducted by the Massachusetts Institute of Technology (MIT) Center for Sports Innovation, Cambridge, MA. Most tests were conducted by MIT students—members of their very successful cycling team—who used a wind tunnel to come to its conclusions.

Facts from the MIT study:

- 75% of the drag experienced during cycling is caused by the resistance of the rider's body to the air.

- The bicycle itself accounts for 15-20% of overall drag.
- A wheel with a deeper rim than 50mm made virtually no difference for the average rider. Note that I said "average rider." At the speeds attained by elite cyclists, more sophisticated wheels including a rear-wheel disk do save important seconds.

- A non-aero helmet creates four (4) times the drag of a non-aero set of wheels. In other words, an aerodynamic helmet is actually more important than aero wheels.

- Proper affixing of the race number is important.

- If you have a bicycle with round tubing, racing with your water bottle is actually more aerodynamic than leaving it off. Racing with your water bottle on the seat tube is more aerodynamic than with it on the down tube.

- Racing with gloves causes more drag than racing gloveless.

Specific time savings over a 40 kilometer time trial course based on measured data:

- Six (6) seconds saved for optimized aerodynamic position on the bike
- Five (5) seconds saved for racing with a water bottle as opposed to not taking it along.
- Four (4) seconds saved for an aerodynamic helmet over a standard cycling helmet.
- Three (3) seconds saved for an aerodynamic bicycle frame.
- Two (2) seconds saved for using aerodynamic wheels
- One (1) second saved for streamlining of the bicycle cables, brakes, etc.

How We Can Benefit From The MIT Study:

- ***The biggest bang for the buck is finding an optimized aerodynamic position on your bicycle. That means using your optimal current position as the starting point.*** In other words, have your position "tweaked" by a professional fitter. When you buy your bicycle, ask if they have a program for re-fitting you to your bike as you progress in your racing.

One of the best examples of this is American professional rider, Tom Danielson, who rides for Garmin-Slipstream and is a past Tour of Georgia winner. Tom's position is tweaked in a wind tunnel quite regularly (as most professional racers are) and the resultant data showed that his optimal position was with his body slightly raised, hand and forearm position retracted, and elbows widened. Tests were conducted measuring the power output required to sustain a speed of 50 kilometers per hour (31.1 mph) on a flat road with a headwind. Amazingly, the power required with his previously wind-tunnel tested (and very successful) position on the bike was 353 watts. After the changes were implemented, Danielson required only 315 watts of generated power to hold the same speed – that's 38 watts less than before! In other words, for the same amount of effort that he previously expended, he can generate more power and go faster.

- If you have the choice of spending $150 for an aerodynamic helmet versus $2,200 for a rear disk wheel and front 80 mm wheel, the helmet choice is not only much more cost effective, but also saves twice the time of the latter choice for the average rider.

- Ride with your water bottle during a time trial race. On my time trial bike, I have only one bottle cage, and it is mounted on the seat tube for optimized aerodynamics.

- Compete with a dedicated time trial bike.

- Glue your number to the back of your racing kit rather than affixing it with safety pins. I use Elmer's Craft Bond™ multi-purpose spray adhesive. Not only is the racing number more aerodynamic, but it alleviates the distraction of the sound of paper flapping about as is so often the case with pinned numbers.

The absolute minimum piece of equipment which is necessary to race a time trial is a set of clip-on aero bars. You will turn a faster time using aero bars than riding on the drops of a standard set of handlebars.

If you don't think a small amount of time saved is significant, know that in a very important time trial race in which I participated, three of us were within 4/10ths of 1 second apart!

If you want to run the fastest possible time, assuming adequate training and technique, here is what you need:

1. A dedicated time trial bike with an expert fitting to find your optimal position.

2. A time trial helmet.

3. A set of aerodynamic wheels – I race the Zipp 999 set (80mm front, disk rear); ideally with tubular tires properly inflated for the road conditions at the race venue.

4. A one-piece skin suit.

5. Booties to cover your shoes.

6. A water bottle mounted on the seat tube (round tube frames).

7. No gloves.

8. Fixative to glue on your racing number.

Recently, I personally tested the aerodynamics I am recommending here. It proved that proper equipment and position on the bike are imperative to winning.

I was riding with one of my training partners, Darren Harris, a triathlete. He rides a beautifully equipped Cervelo P3™ time trial bike, and has had his position on the bike professionally fitted. I was riding a Specialized Roubaix™ with 58 millimeter carbon wheels and tubular tires. Darren and I would start coasting down a bridge side by side. Darren was on his aero bars and I was riding on my drops. We would assure that our speeds were exactly the same, and then we would begin to coast. Darren would literally leave me like I was standing still.

A week later, we did the same experiment. Darren was now riding on a Cervelo road bike, and I was on the same one used the previous week. When we would coast down the bridge, Darren and I would stay even. We also tried the experiments on flat roads where we would achieve the same speed, stop pedaling, and see who coasted the best. The results were the same as the bridge tests. It was an incredible demonstration of the difference between and aerodynamic bike being ridden by a rider properly fitted to the bike versus a standard road bike also properly fitted.

Bicycle Fittings and Aerodynamics:

For the potential gold medal winner: If you were to check the power you generate riding in a comfortable, non-aerodynamic position, you might be surprised to discover that you actually generate more power (as measured in watts on a power meter) in that position than you do in your optimal aerodynamic position. The fact that you generate less power but go faster demonstrates the importance of aerodynamics, and the resultant proper positioning on the bike.

The #1 most important investment you can make to enhance your cycling and make it truly enjoyable every day is to have a professional fitting. A professional fitting is substantially more involved than the typical "quick fitting" at the shop where you purchased your bike. Usually, the shop will to do no more than the saddle fore/aft and height adjustments and, perhaps, a turn up or down of your handlebars. So often, those simplistic adjustments are done incorrectly. The result is that you will not be riding to your potential.

I had the typical "after sale" fitting on my first bike. It felt comfortable, and I was riding well with it. What did I know? Four months later, I received a Christmas present of a professional bicycle fitting. It took about two hours, was captured on video, used sophisticated equipment, and was accomplished by a fitter trained by John Cobb, a man who has worked with Lance Armstrong.

The stationary trainer upon which the bicycle was mounted was equipped with a power meter to record subtle differences in power output. The fitting included not only adjustments to the bike, but also included a new stem and shoe/cleat adjustments with shims to compensate for a leg- length discrepancy. It was interesting to watch the progress on a TV monitor that graphically demonstrated with each adjustment how I increased my ability to generate more power as displayed on the power meter. It was awesome!

The bottom line: At the end of the fitting, I was generating substantially more power on each stroke, my position was very comfortable, and, once I got on the road with my newly fitted bike, I was suddenly winning sprints at the end of club rides!

Ideally, if you can afford and want the absolute optimum fit to your bike, purchase a custom-made bicycle, made-to-measure. My two custom-made bicycles were a delight to ride right out of their boxes.

My Guru time trial bike required two fittings to find my aerodynamic "sweet spot" and comfort zone. The result was I went under the state record for the 5K time trial the first time I rode the bike in competition. Most of the shops that do professional fittings will do future adjustments at no charge.

Now, for those of you who are really hard core with bank accounts to match, there are fittings available in wind tunnels such as the one a 58 year old masters cyclist friend of mine used last year in Texas to have his already-very-efficient (he is a past Canadian national and North American masters time trial champion) aerodynamic position tweaked even more. The upshot was that he turned an incredible time of 52:56 for 40 kilometers at the 2008 USCF Florida State Time Trial Championships – that's an average of 28+ mph for just less than 25 miles!

If you simply want to enter bicycle races with a participatory attitude to have some fun, you can disregard the above information. If you want to "make the podium" and ideally win, you probably will not be able to accomplish that, at least in my state, unless you heed the above recommendations. If you want a sport that "feels good," forget about time trialing – it is incredibly painful when done correctly! It is delightful pain however!

 # CHAPTER 10...

INTRODUCTION TO TRAINING

It is never too late to start a new sport—especially cycling which many of us did as children and loved for the freedom it gave us. Although training on my bicycle for racing gives me a lot more pain that I had when I rode around my home town in my youth, I have a great appreciation for the fact that I can do this in my late 60s and am looking forward to continuing on to my 80s.

The rest of this story is how Sandy's experience can help you get into great shape and mature your bicycle training in order to win the gold medals.

"I came to cycling quite late in life at the age of 64 when my fiancée, Rosie, appeared at my house with two bicycles and announced that we were going for a bicycle ride. She had no way of knowing what she was about to unleash!"

Sandy was a couch potato at that time—at least by my definition. We met through Match.com and I had put in my profile that I did not want one of those! After a half-dozen dates, I decided to get him out of his house and on the road. I was tired of hearing about how great an athlete he was in the past and I was training for a triathlon. All he was doing was weight lifting because he had plantar fasciitis and it was very painful just to walk.

"Rosie and I went on a picnic and the bike she brought was an old Kabuki. The chain was slipping, but I took to it like a duck to water. Several months later, I treated myself to a new bike, asked Rosie to marry me, and got involved with riding with the St. Pete Bike Club in the summer of 2004."

"I am now a 69 year old avid, master cyclist. To say that I am passionate about cycling is an understatement. Currently, I am the USCF Florida State time trial and road race champion, and the current Florida State Seniors Games 5 & 10K time trial champion. I hold state age group records in both of the latter events. I train on the bicycle about 25-27 hours weekly and lift weights about three times a week. I just completed a complete calendar year without missing a single day of training (15,559 miles). You have to love to work if you want to win!"

This is Sandy and I want to tell you that, in my 30s and 40s, I competed as an elite-level runner for the Shore AC in New Jersey, and coached some very successful runners. Among my teammates was the famous Dr. George Sheehan, cardiologist, prolific author, medical editor for Runner's World magazine, and national age group record holder at 1500 meters.

With consistency in your training, dedication to riding the miles it takes to make yourself strong, and the spirit to go over and beyond what is necessary, you will become a winner. Envisioning yourself on the top will not get you there. Doing your personal best every time you go out to race and setting goals for every day will insure your success.

Try not to compare yourself to others but know your competition. What they ride and wear may not be what you need to beat them. However, neither underestimate your competition nor believe that you cannot go out and win on any particular day. Learn how to do minor repairs on your bicycle, keep it clean and properly lubricated, eat well and rest after a hard day—but be on your bike every day and put in the miles to make you stronger. It is the engine that counts and it does not matter if someone is racing with pedals with straps and a tee-shirt. It gets down to grit and determination and a lot of pain to win a race!

 # CHAPTER II...

GOALS AND DREAMS

Sandy has a lot of interesting experiences under his belt and he likes to associate a story from his past with almost every topic we discuss for this book. His stories let you get to know him and so we are being selective in those we share so we do not overly bore you if you are solely interested in getting to the guts of the training.

When it comes to goal setting, Sandy was a winner in his career as an airline pilot, a motorcycle cop, and as the VP-Sales for SimCom International, a company that he helped build. He also enjoyed great success at his various hobbies such as skydiving where he attained his "Master Skydiver" certification in a record few months, playing in chess tournaments, amateur radio, competitive bass fishing, martial arts, golf, tennis, photography, target shooting, and collecting all manners of things.

Sandy started working as a caddy at the local golf course at the tender age of eight. He also delivered newspapers and mowed lawns. At the age of 15, he was trying to figure out a way to finance a car and came up with the idea of starting his own egg business. He established his first goal to buy a new car on his own.

He went door-to-door soliciting customers for his product – fresh eggs delivered to their door every Saturday morning. He contracted with a local Purina farmer in Stockton, California, and would pick up the eggs in bulk every Friday evening. He would then box and deliver them to his customers on Saturday morning. His route kept expanding and he eventually added the delivery of fresh chickens after contracting with a local butcher. His business was so successful, that he was able to almost immediately replace is 1948 Mercury coupe for which he had paid $100 with a beautiful, two-year-old Ford sedan.

Some of us have to be prodded and pushed by family and friends into setting goals for our own sake and others. Those like Sandy, find it is a natural thing to do. No one else is responsible for their success. They plan their work and work the plan and succeed in whatever they set their mind to do.

Setting the goal of riding 70 minutes on his bicycle trainer in the garage every day of his broken-neck agony while in the hard brace helped keep Sandy focused on what he was going to do after his neck got better: Win the State of Florida time trial and road races and break all the records.

So, before we get into the meat and potatoes of goal setting, here is a little story Sandy wanted to share with you:

"When my career at Eastern Airlines ended so abruptly, I was stunned. I loved flying more than I can express here, but I can assure you I would have flown for no pay if I could have kept working for Eastern."

"What the actual motivation was that caused me to jump into a plan and set up some goals and become a pilot so fast was surprising even to me as a young, married man who had never been in a small airplane before. It was serendipity that led me to flying and goal setting, planning, and working at it that made me a success."

"When I was a police officer--motorcycle cop, my career goal at the time was to become an FBI agent. In those days, 1961-1966, the requirements to be a special agent were either a law degree or being a certified public accountant. As an engineering student, I loved math, but being a CPA did not sound exciting to me so I chose law as my route to the FBI and I was attending law school to accomplish my mission."

"One beautiful, California Sunday morning, I parked my police motorcycle in front of police headquarters, and, as I passed the area that housed the police dispatcher, I noticed that he was manipulating an interesting looking device. Being an engineer by schooling, I expressed immediate interest, and the dispatcher explained that he was taking flying lessons, and the device he held was a computer used to solve various flying related calculations."

"The dispatcher went on to explain that his goal was to become an airline pilot and further explained that, due to the Vietnam War, military pilots were not being released, and, with the rapid growth of the airlines, it was possible to become an airline pilot with civilian training. He told me that the minimum licenses required were a commercial pilot's license and an instrument rating. Prior to working on those licenses, it was necessary to be a licensed as a private pilot."

"I told him that I had never been in a light aircraft, and would love to accompany him on a flight sometime. He said, "Meet me at the Palo Alto airport after the shift, and we'll go flying."

"Later that day, I met him at the airport and he gave me a tour of the Piper Cherokee 140 that we were going to fly. He further expanded upon his goal to become an airline pilot. We finally took off, and an incredible feeling overcame me as we broke ground. A large heart must have formed over my head, because I found that I immediately fell, head-over-heels in love with flying. By the end of the flight, I said, "I'm going to become an airline pilot!"

"The next day, I appeared at Nystrom Aviation at the very same airport and announced to a chap behind the desk: 'I want to get a private pilots license, commercial license and instrument rating.' The reply was, 'slow down kid! Let's just sign you up for your first lesson!'"

"I started taking lessons with a vengeance, and studied everything I could about flying and aviation. I told all of my fellow police officers that I was going to become an airline pilot, but most scoffed at me saying, 'yeah, right! Maybe in your dreams!"

"Although the story has some other interesting twists and turns, the bottom line is that I finished all of my ratings in 11 months, and applied with three airlines as a pilot: Eastern, United and TWA—only one of which is still flying. Amazingly, I was offered a position at each of them with a paltry 226 hours of total flying time! The typical pilot has thousands of hours when hired so I considered myself very lucky, indeed."

The lesson from this story is that the seemingly impossible can happen, but it cannot happen unless you have a goal and a plan on what it will take to begin and end, and are willing to work hard to accomplish it. Luck really has nothing to do with it.

Sandy loved every second of the 25 years spent flying with Eastern Airlines. It was an amazing journey in life that started with a goal and a plan to accomplish a serendipitous dream--a dream that many others thought to be unattainable.

CHAPTER 12...

SETTING YOUR GOALS

Success emanates from setting and achieving goals. Success does not happen because of fate nor does it happen because you wish it to. Goals enhance our lives by being a template we can follow that becomes tried and true. I firmly believe that a person without goals is simply going through the motions of life missing one of the greatest enhancements to his or her self-fulfillment—setting, focusing on, and achieving meaningful goals.

Let me define what I mean by a "goal" in that not everyone shares my definition. To me the desire and intention to accomplish something in the future cannot be considered a goal unless the goal is defined by very specific time parameters. For example, if I were to say, "I want to learn a foreign language," that is not a goal— simply a desire. However, if I say, "I intend to learn Spanish prior to leaving for Spain in June," that is a goal.

Every good sales person has to set goals based upon opportunities; forecast (set the expectation) as to when the goal will be met; and plan his or her work to meet or exceed the goals. I am sure that most of you in business have heard the expression: Plan the work and work your plan. This is a great principle when you are setting goals for your ultimate gold medal wins.

I had numerous goals for 2008, but for the purpose of this piece, I will speak only of setting my goals as they related to cycling – an activity for which I have a deep passion as an ex-sales executive and inveterate record keeper.

As an example, my cycling goals for 2008 were divided into two categories: "competitive" and "other." My competitive goals were to win the United States Cycling Federation, Florida State Time Trial and Road Race championships. In addition, my goals were to win the 5K and 10K Time Trial races at the Florida State Senior Games Championships. I accomplished all of those.

The most challenging goal however, fell into the category of "other" cycling goals. My goal was to train on my bicycle every single day of the calendar year without missing one day and in doing so having no "fluff" mileage days. In other words, I would not consider my goal accomplished if I simply went out and rode a very few miles so that I wouldn't miss a day.

To me, a rest day on the bicycle is an easy 35 mile spin. I love to get on my bike every day and it doesn't matter if it is cold or wet, sunny, or cloudy. The miles add up as I am having fun.

Achieving the "no-missed-days" goal was not easy. I found myself training in some rather miserable weather, and sometimes it was quite inconvenient to work in rides while away from home. To accomplish the latter, I never left home without one of my bicycles.

Now, please don't think I am excessive or compulsive by what I am about to tell you. Just understand that when I set a goal, I take it very seriously. There are many ways to rationalize a missed goal, but I'm not interested—a goal is a goal, and it is to be accomplished!

In mid-December last year, a dentist appointment revealed that a tooth needed to be extracted. The dentist wanted to perform the procedure within a couple of days due to the nature of the problem. When she informed me that a tooth extraction would require a couple of days of not riding a bicycle (apparently the clot needs to form at the extraction site and vigorous exercise does not enhance that need), I really had to think about having it done. Rather than give up on my goal, I scheduled the appointment for the extraction after the first of the year.

Another impediment to my goal was a scheduled surgery on the 22nd of December at 9AM. I was on my trainer (a device to which a bicycle can be attached and ridden indoors) at 5AM in the morning so as not to miss that day. The surgeon knows me quite well in that I'm a poster boy for skin cancer, and although he would love me to take off two weeks after a surgery, he simply now uses extra thick sutures, and keeps them in place for an extra week. I have him well trained!

I rode 15,823.68 miles in 2008 and my average weekly mileage was 303.47. My next goal will be for 16,000 miles in 2009 for which I am on target. The date I achieve the goal is irrelevant (as long it is during the specified year) in that I will be out there achieving it as planned and nothing will stop me!

I am retired and have the time to be in the saddle for four to five hours per day. Some people have to work and, like Rosie, choose to have a life other than being on a bicycle! When you are setting your goals for bicycling, doing your first 25 mile ride may be a tremendous goal as it was for her. It was a trip from home to our neighborhood's Millennium Park and through it, up the Pinellas Trail to Taylor Park and through it, up to Clearwater and the end of the paved trail, and back through the parks and home.It was a big deal for her and she called her son, Ian, a retired professional triathlete and Team U.S.A. member, and bragged on herself. Everyone needs to do that when they set and achieve a goal.

When you start to increment your time on the bike and the miles you put in, you will find that time flies by as you pedal away. Finding friends and joining a bicycling club that has regular rides is a great way to improve your abilities to do longer distances. Keep focused on the fact that the more you ride the stronger you become and the closer you get to your goal of winning races. The old saying, "Practice Makes Perfect" definitely applies to biking!

CHAPTER 13...

PLANNING THE YEAR'S TRAINING

If you are interested in racing whether it be running or cycling, it is very important to have a plan and goals for the entire year. Let me use my last year's plan as an example.

For 2008, my goals were to win the USCF time trial and road race championships which were to be contested over a period of two (2) weeks around the first half of June. My second goal was to win the Florida State Senior Games time trial and road race championships to be contested the second week of December.

My racing goals dictated that I reach peak form twice in the year. Typically, reaching two peaks in a year is the most that one can hope to achieve without risking injury, burnout or getting sick. After reaching a peak, six (6) weeks is about the maximum time one can hope to maintain peak form.

I divided the year into two, six-month segments, and each of those segments was divided into three (3) two-month segments:

1. Rest and Recovery
2. Base & Strength Building
3. Peaking

The first phase, "Rest and Recovery" was necessary in that I was coming off a peak from the previous December. During that phase of my training, I kept my mileage basically the same, which for me is around 300-350 miles a week with an occasional foray over 400 miles. I simply rode my bike and had fun. I would engage in about one fast club ride per week, but I was mostly spinning the rest of the time. After two months of that routine, I moved into the base and strength building phase of my training with the feeling that my "battery" was fully charged.

The second phase, "Base & Strength Building" follows on quite naturally. I believe that masters athletes should weight train 12 months out of the year. The only time I weight train my legs in a serious manner, however, is during my strength-building segment where I incorporate 20 repetition squats adding 5 pounds of weight every week. During this period, I continue to build my base taking occasional rides of up to 100 miles. I also do two fast rides per week as I continue to prepare for the difficult two months to come – peaking! When you have built a substantial base, the peaking process is much more readily accomplished. Without a substantial base, peaking would be analogous to trying to hone a fine edge on a very thin piece of steel.

Finally, the last phase, "Peaking" is done in the last two months leading up to the important race(s). During the peaking period, I start my interval training and also incorporate hill training and/or bridge repeats. During this phase, I work up to three (3) to four (4) hard rides per week. I also engage in local races as much as possible in that no training can possibly replicate an actual race situation. Racing is a great way to attain peak form.

When I completed my goal races, I started the next six-month segment – a repeat of the first one.

If your racing plans call for only one peak per year, then simply spend more time in the base/strength building portion of your schedule. The peaking process must still be two months duration.

My philosophy of each of us being an experiment of one holds true. I missed no days of training in 2008. Rather than take actual rest days, I have found that "active rest" works best for me. My typical rest day is

35 easy miles just enjoying riding my bicycle. I typically do that with a training partner. I feel much better the next day than I do if I don't ride at all.

The professionals do the same thing. At the 2009 Tour de France, there was a rest day scheduled after three hard days of racing in the Pyrenees Mountains. In an interview with Levi Leipheimer, the reporter said to Levi, "I bet you are looking forward to the rest day." Levi enthusiastically answered, "Yes!" The reporter asked what he was going to do on the rest day. Levi replied, "Ride about two to three hours."

Finally, I train with athletes who have incredibly complicated programs that they pay substantial amounts of money for. Candidly, I sometimes wonder if the complications are simply a way for the provider of the training plan to justify the hundreds of dollars per month spent by the client to receive the coaching.

Training is not complicated: you simply stress the body and it adapts when you rest it. If you train it harder, it adapts to a higher level. When I was taking golf lessons, I would over think and complicate everything. The best advice I ever had was when one pro told me, "Golf is just hitting a stick with a ball." Here for example is a simplistic description of the tapering process prior to a major race – I call it "Tapering for Dummies:

- Ride hard.
- Ride really hard.
- Ride really, really hard.
- Get tired.
- Ride easy.
- Ride easy again.
- Ride even easier.
- Ride easy; eat a good dinner; Get a good night's sleep.
- Kick butt in the race the next morning.

WE ARE EACH AN EXPERIMENT OF ONE...

We are going to begin with the techniques which work for most people. Understand that each of us is unique, hence *WE ARE EACH AN EXPERIMENT OF ONE*. What might work quite effectively for me might need a bit of "tweaking" to work for you.

To improve one's performance in an aerobic sport requires a training effort that challenges the body, gives it adequate recovery and rest time from the training, and adapts to the subsequent processes that consistently improves the body's overall performance.

When the body is challenged through proper training, it adapts to the effort by becoming stronger and more efficient. In an aerobic sport, the body's ability to consume oxygen (VO2max) is increased as is its ability to deal with lactic acid leading to an increase in Lactic Threshold (LT).

I am not going to get too technical so let me say that when you reach your LT the body starts having difficulty dissipating the build up of lactic acid and it begins to hurt. Obviously, if you can increase your body's ability to deal with lactic acid, you can go faster longer.

Although an athlete can typically attain his or her genetic potential VO2max in as little as a year, the exciting news is that it takes many years of training to attain one's optimal Lactic Threshold; hence one can expect to see years of improvement from training.

The biggest mistake that I observe in some cyclists is doing the same thing all the time. For example, here in the St. Petersburg, FL area, there are clubs rides every weekday morning at 8:30 a.m. The rides typically follow the same route at the same speeds, and often have the same participants. Many riders wonder why they have no improvement and in some cases actually experience degradation in performance. The reason of course is that the body simply adapts to the same routine and has no reason to improve.

If you do group rides, set a goal of being in the front of the peloton with consistency and, when you are just getting comfortable, move up to the next fastest group.

Always try to go beyond your comfort zone. If you have difficulty being in a group and hold back because you are fearful of getting into a wreck, that is understandable. However, if you are always at the back of the group, you stand a better chance of getting dropped. It may feel comfortable there, but the minute you go around a curve or stop at a traffic light, you stand the chance of getting left behind due to the accordion effect of the group. If you stay up front and on the wheel of the leader, it gives you a great workout and chance to do some pulling at your own speed.

CHAPTER 15...

INTERVAL TRAINING FOR CYCLISTS

When I was a high school distance runner in the 50's, the sport of track and field was not only seasonal, but the training, unlike today, was also seasonal for the runners. Training would often commence just a couple of weeks prior to the season, and hence without much of a base from which to sharpen. How could one go from no training to running a competitive mile in just a few weeks? It was through intense interval training. Interval training is the quickest and most effective route to successful racing performance, and is, ideally, commenced after a substantial build-up of base mileage.

In those days, Wes Santee was the premier American miler and our coach would put us through what he called, "The Wes Santee Workout." It was excruciating and often caused shin splints and other miscellaneous aches and pains. For those of you who are curious as to what comprised the workout, it was as follows:

- A Two (2) mile warm-up followed by stretching.

- Seven (7), 440-yard dashes at a pace dictated by the coach.

- Seven (7), 220-yard dashes at a pace dictated by the coach.

- A one (1) mile time trial.

- A two (2) mile warm down.

The rest intervals were quite short and it was often rather difficult to hold down any food that might be my stomach. I sometimes found myself kneeling and retching in the showers after the workout.

If one survived, it worked great! I was personally able to run a PR of 4:36 for the mile, running only briefly before and during the track season. In later years, I coached runners and interval training was a very important part of their training whether they were preparing for a mile track race or a marathon.

To achieve your full potential as a cyclist, proper interval training is a "must" addition to your training regimen. Incorporating regular interval training into your peaking routine during the last six to eight (6-8) weeks leading up to a very important competition is invaluable if you want to win. This will be covered in more depth in the section on training for racing.

Most athletes appreciate that interval training enhances one's VO2max (the ability to consume and utilize oxygen) and lactate threshold (the exercise intensity at which lactic acid starts to accumulate in the blood stream). However, many athletes are not aware of the importance of training one's nervous system for racing. Racing a time trial to one's maximum potential can be quite a shock to the nervous system, and if you are not used to training intensely (interval training), the body will balk when you ask it to perform to maximum efforts in a race.

In summary, interval training improves your ability to consume oxygen, allows you to race at a more intense level before the body is negatively affected by lactic acid, and prepares your nervous system for the rigors of high-level racing.

My favorite cycling interval training routine is simple, but incredibly effective. The workout has enabled me to break the 5K, 10K, and 20K Florida State Time Trial records in my age group. As an aside, a recent study showed short intervals to be not only an effective training regimen for short time trial racing (5K & 10K), but was also shown to be very effective for longer time trial races such as the 40 kilometer distance.

The workout is as follows:

- A one (1) hour warm-up.
- Six (6), one-half (½) mile intervals.
- One (1) hour warm down.

The "warm-up" is the same one that I use when I am going to race a time trial:

The warm-up takes approximately one hour. Spin at an easy-to-moderate pace for the first 30 minutes. During the second 30 minutes, commence brief pick-ups (increases in speed and intensity of riding) at planned race pace starting with 30 second pickups, followed by easy spinning for a few minutes, and work up to one-minute pick-ups at race pace. Finally, I do a couple of 15 second sprints at a few mph above proposed race pace. You want to feel some lactic acid build-up in your legs, which you will dissipate between pick-up efforts.

An interesting demonstration as to how important the lactic acid generating pickups are is as follows: The next time you are warming up for a fast club ride, do a couple of pick-ups that generate some lactic acid build-up in your legs. You will probably note that on about the third one, you will no longer feel any lactic acid for the same effort.

If you race or do a fast club ride without warming up with speed pick-ups in advance, you will undoubtedly experience discomfort early on due to lactic acid build-up.

The intervals are accomplished at a speed of five to ten percent (5%-10%) faster than the proposed race pace. If, for example, you are training to do a time trial averaging a pace of 25 mph, do your intervals at 26.25 to 27.5 mph.

Another important consideration of interval training is your "rest interval." In your first couple of interval sessions, I suggest that you allow yourself to feel "reasonably recovered" prior to commencing your next interval. I utilize a heart-rate monitor, and I feel fully recovered when my heart rate reaches 120 or lower. As you continue the peaking process, it is important to shorten the recovery interval to more replicate a race situation.

Doing intervals on a road that runs North and South here in Tampa Bay, Florida, we get a lot of practice in adverse wind conditions because the winds are usually from those directions. As the weeks of intervals accumulate, my typical rest interval becomes just the time it takes me to slow my bike, make a U-turn and get back to the starting point (the ending point for the previous interval) for the next interval. That is often under 30 seconds between intervals. The key concept is that you don't want to feel recovered when you start your next interval which leads to a better training effect.

Some trainees are tempted to do their intervals only downwind because they feel so much better. Don't fall into that trap. It is important to do intervals into the wind—some of my most important time trial events have been on very windy days where the first half of the race was into the wind. Train for the wind!

Many trainees have a tendency to start slowing as they approach the finish point of the interval. It will be often be quite painful, especially in your last couple of intervals, to hold your planned speed as you approach the end, but at that point you must fight to hold your pace until you are completely through the finish point.

Keep in mind that we are each an experiment of one. As you get closer to your maximum peak, you might want to experiment with doing a second set of intervals in the last couple of weeks of your peaking process. If you decide to try a second set, spin easily for approximately 15 minutes after completing the first set, and then start the second set of six (6) intervals. If you find that you cannot complete any of the intervals with good form, or hold your target speed to the end of the interval, stop the workout and do your warm down. Train for success—not failure. Two sets of intervals makes for a very challenging workout. It does, however, toughen you both physically and mentally—both vital for successful time trialing! Finally, do a warm down ride of ideally an hour of easy spinning.

Remember that interval training is training for racing. Be aware of your form during the intervals. It is very easy to break form during the latter stages of a painful interval session. During the interval, check your position on the bike. Your grip should be relaxed, your knees should be close to the top tube, your face should be relaxed (the pain notwithstanding), your pedal stroke should be smooth and symmetrical (not mashing down on the pedals), and you should be breathing properly.

A good technique utilized by some top riders to achieve their optimal aerodynamic position is to imagine trying to touch the top tube of the bicycle with your belly. Do not get in the habit of looking down as you tire during the interval—even the pros fall victim to that bad habit. If you do, you will be sticking the point of a large aero helmet into the airstream—not a good idea!

Finally, you might try a technique given to me by an ex-cycling Olympian as I mentioned in "Racing a Time Trial." It is also an excellent technique for interval training. We have a section of the Pinellas Trail where we usually do our intervals. There is a palm tree on one end and a series of pipes at the other end. We use those as our race markers. You can pick an object down the road such as a sign, tree, house or whatever you have available and imagine that it is a large magnet pulling you towards it. It really makes you concentrate.

When you are tearing down the road in a time trial, you will be always looking toward the finish line and the usual tent that is there. It is amazing how much faster you can go when you see that you are close to the finish line. The same applies when you are racing.

Proper breathing is something we tend to forget, but is very important in any physical activity we do and is especially true in training and racing. I'm sure most of you are aware of the fact that the most efficient breathing method is belly breathing—not chest breathing. With belly breathing, your belly rather than your chest rises. It is the most efficient means of taking in maximum oxygen utilizing the fewest muscles. The more muscles you use, the more oxygen you needlessly consume, and the harder your heart has to work.

When I commence my interval training in my peaking process, I do one session per week, and, as I get closer to the event for which I am peaking, I do two sessions per week. Remember that improvement is made during your rest (recovery) days when the body compensates for the stress to which you have subjected it—not your work days. If you don't rest, you simply do not improve. It is vital, especially for the masters athlete, that an interval session be followed by either a complete day off the bike or my favorite approach of active rest—an easy spin day.

My rest-day is typically two and one-half hours of easy spinning. I find that my body actually feels better the day after an active rest day rather than a full day off the bike. Discover what works best for you.

In summary, interval training is one of the most effective ways to train for racing. Do them during the peaking process the few weeks prior to the time you want to reach maximum form. Do them once or twice a week with adequate warm-up and warm-down. Do them with proper form, and finally, have an adequate rest day the day after your interval session.

Finally, when you have a planned interval training day, as the Nike™ slogan says, "Just Do It!" It is very easy to talk one's self out of a session of difficult intervals. If you allow yourself to miss a planned interval workout, it will be easier to talk yourself into slowing down during a race.

# CHAPTER 16...

WEIGHT TRAINING

Weight training for the masters athlete takes on a high-level of importance in the scheme of things when you are trying to become a winner. As we age, we tend to gain fat and lose muscle mass and women, especially, have a harder time trimming down to get into racing shape. Men have a higher percentage of muscle mass than women throughout their lives, hence women typically find it more difficult to lose weight. Not only that, men have a 10%-15% advantage in their BMR (basic metabolic rate) than women.

It has been proven that weight training which increases muscle mass raises the basic metabolic rate at which we burn fat. Turning your body into a leaner, more muscular engine contributes to healthy bones and makes you a stronger, faster cyclist. Replacing 10 pounds of fat with 10 pounds of muscle, you can expect to expend more than 500 more kilo-calories when at rest. Just being "in shape" can burn off calories without you being aware of it.

For every pound of new muscle, your body will burn an extra 60 calories per day. Three extra pounds of muscles burns as much calories in your workout as running 25 miles per week. This is really important in that women tend to spend less time on the bike and more in the house with taking care of children, cooking, cleaning, and, otherwise, not getting to the gym. We have a gym in our house which Rosie recognized as good for both of us only since she started racing.

A regular routine of proper weight training can and does reverse the process of continuously having to work at losing weight. My routine in racing season while I am peaking is to do a "brief" workout in our gym two days per week for 20 minutes. This is to work at "pushing" my upper body. At the age of 69, I have approximately 4% body fat, so I can attest to the results of proper weight training. Weight training will not only help you maintain muscle and bone mass, but will quite simply make you look and feel better. Needless to say, it will make you stronger and a stronger athlete is a better performer.

I have always been a proponent of weight training. In my younger years, I approached weight training from more of a body-building perspective. When I returned to competitive athletics in my mid-thirties, I transitioned to weight training programs more oriented towards enhancing my sports performance. I don't think you will find a world-class athlete who does not incorporate weight training into his or her training regimen. On a personal level, I have been training with weights for over 40 years consecutively.

However, in my first phase of lifting when I was in my teens, I had the mistaken impression that more is better. I had a barbell set in my bedroom and I attacked my workouts with a vengeance. Reading muscle magazines, I dreamed about being stronger and more appealing like the guy in the ads on the beach. However, I started with 9 3/8 inch arms. My goal was to get to monstrous arms—16 inch arms looked like a great goal in those pre-steroid days when you had to work with your natural body to get them in shape.

I would often work out with weights six (6) days per week, and have sessions as long as a several hours in duration. When I transitioned from "cosmetic" weight training to a program to enhance my running, I still worked out three times per week, exercising each body part at each session. I was fortunate enough to discover arguably the best book ever written on the subject of weight training: Stuart McRobert's, *Beyond Brawn*. The book changed my weight training life by not only enhancing my results, but also allowing me to do so in substantially less time. I would highly recommend that you make this bible of weight training a part of your library. The author's website is www.hardgainer.com and you can find everything that he offers at that site.

Many so-called experts would counsel a cyclist that weight training must be dedicated to cycling-specific muscles. I would argue that the muscles needed for cycling are exercised sufficiently during the act of cycling. Do not, however, infer from the previous sentence that muscles used in cycling do not have to be exercised apart from the act of cycling. I believe that those muscles, in addition to every other muscle, must be weight-trained. What I'm proposing is that, regardless of your sport, your program can basically be the same.

A tutorial on weight training is a book in itself. For this book, I am simply sharing my experiences and will give you a summary of the basic principles and guidelines that will allow you to preserve and develop muscle mass and enhance your performance on the bike.

One of the ways that you will spend less time without compromising your results will be through utilizing "compound" rather than "isolation" exercises. The compound weight training exercise is comprised of multiple-joint movements; isolation weight training involves single-joint movements. An example of a compound exercise, and one of the most effective exercises that one can perform, is the squat. When a squat is performed, multiple joints and muscle groups are involved; i.e., the quadriceps, gluteus and erectus muscles—very important muscles for the cyclist. An example of an isolation exercise is the leg extension which involves only one joint and targets only the quadriceps muscles.

The most overused isolation exercises are the various triceps extension and press down exercises. Your triceps will be exercised adequately when you perform various compound-pressing movements such as the bench press and overhead press.

Probably the most startling revelation of all is the fact that great progress can be made—and, in many cases, better progress—by exercising each body part once as opposed to multiple times per week. The keys to successful results are:

- Regularity
- Intensity
- Progression.

Regularity is having some type of schedule and sticking to it. Have a plan and goal and do your best to work your plan.

Intensity should be self-explanatory. If you do not exercise with reasonable intensity, the body has no reason to adapt and your progress either ceases or you regress.

By *progression*, I mean that one should add some weight to each exercise every week. I will address that in more depth below.

The most important group of exercises that you must incorporate into your routine(s), are the "core movements." These core movements are the compound exercises that must be the foundation of any successful program. They are comprised of various compound leg/back movements such as squats, leg presses, various types of dead-lifts, and upper body exercises such as the bench press, pull-up and pull-down movements, various types of rowing and shrug movements, and the overhead press. The typical routine will have between two to five (2-5) movements.

It is also important to incorporate secondary exercises into your routine that works the abdominals, calves, neck, and lower back.

Exercises can be spread over multiple workouts during the week, or every body part can be exercised on the same day. I enjoy the multiple workout variety which I find to be quite convenient in that I have a fully-equipped, home gym. I typically do my weight workouts on my cycling recovery days.

My favorite approach is what I call the "push/pull" method. On one day, I will do pushing, compound exercises such as the bench press and the overhead press, and on the next workout I will incorporate the pulling movements—rows, pull-downs, etc.

Just as in cycling, progress is made through the adaptation process. Muscle tissue is torn down and the body repairs the tissue and adds extra tissue in preparation for the next workout. The bottom line is that the muscles get stronger the more you work them.

Let's say that you do bench presses on one workout day and on the next you do overhead presses. The problem is that both workouts utilize the triceps; therefore they don't get the necessary recovery. Hence, the rationale for my push/pull approaches to training. Note: I am not saying that you cannot do those exercises on the same day, but if you do, there is no need to do them again for approximately another week.

Weight training should be accomplished in cycles. Cycles are typically 10-12 weeks in duration. The beginning of the cycle will feel easy in that a weight will be chosen for most exercises in which 12 repetitions can be readily performed. Each week, weight will be added to each exercise—more on heavier exercises such as the squat and less on others. Finally, towards the end of the cycle, at the point at which it is impossible to add further weight without doing less than eight (8) repetitions, it is time to start a new cycle. The new cycle is commenced by cutting back the weight on all exercises approximately 15-20%. It is also a good time to substitute exercises. For example, you might substitute a lateral pull-down exercise with a rowing-type exercise or do an incline bench press versus the standard version.

Once you get into the meat of the program and are doing less than 12 repetitions, I believe in "exercising to failure." That is the point where you either cannot finish the repetition or are incapable of doing another. Be sure to do this safely by incorporating a spotter (training partner) or a device like a Smith Machine which has safety features to capture a barbell when only a partial rep can be completed.

As you progress through multiple cycles over time, you will notice that the point at which you must start a new cycle will be when you are lifting heavier than you were at the end of your last cycle.

I would suggest that at the end of your first cycle, you set a benchmark by doing the following three tests of your strength:

1)   Squat – 135 pounds
2)   Bench Press – 135 pounds
3)   Dead-lift – 150 pounds

Determine what the maximum number of repetitions you can do in each exercise, and record it in your log book. When you finish each cycle, repeat the test—you will be amazed, and quite pleased with the results.

Women should use approximately ½ the poundage of the above amounts for their test.

Keep a log book of your workouts as a reference tool.

I think one of the most valuable exercises that one can perform, is the 20-repetition "breathing squat." When I was lifting weights for the purpose of body building in my twenties, I found it very difficult to make progress. I was the typical ectomorphic body type with a rather slender frame—not the kind of build where muscle is easily added (the mesomorphic body type).

I discovered an incredible system called, ***The Perry Rader Squat System.*** Perry Rader was the founder of one of the first body-building magazines, ***Iron Man***. There is no resemblance to that magazine and the current one that bears its name. Rader published a pamphlet describing his system. His philosophy was, "If you want to build your arms, do squats." He indicated that squats so thoroughly stimulate the whole body, that, when properly executed, the total body makes progress in strength and size.

He promulgated the 20-repetition, breathing squat, which was basically a barbell squat in which three to four (3-4) breaths were taken between each repetition. The system includes five (5) other basic exercises:

1. Bench Press
2. Overhead Press
3. Rows
4. Barbell Curls
5. Calf Raises

It was basically a two- or three-times per week routine. I was delighted when I gained seven (7) pounds of muscle in a couple of months on that regimen. To this day, I do 20-repetition squats when I am not peaking for an event.

While on the subject, the best approach to 20-repetition squats is to perform them once a week, go no lower than upper legs parallel to the ground, and warm up properly prior to doing the 20-repetition work set. I warm up by doing some "free squats" without weights, and then one set of 12 repetitions with 155 pounds. 20-rep squats are hard. Often times when you have completed the 10th rep, it will seem impossible to do another 10—you can (and must) do it! With this particular exercise, I add five (5) pounds per week in weight, until I can absolutely no longer complete 20 reps. I then decrease the weight by about 20% and start another cycle.

It is vital that you keep good form. Do not bend forward as you squat—keep your back straight. Again, do not go lower than upper legs parallel to the ground. As cyclists, we need to guard our knees!

Here is my current, rather effective, but rather simple routine that I can easily complete each day in less than 30 minutes:

Day 1: (Legs & Abdominal Muscles)
Some form of abdominal work – I prefer hanging, leg lifts
    (1)   Squats - Warm-up - set of 12 reps
    (1)   Breathing Squats – Work - set of 20 reps
    (2)   Seated, Calf raises

Day 2: (Chest, Shoulders & Triceps)
    (1)   Bench Press - Warm up - set, of 10-12 reps
    (2)   Sets - Bench Press - Work
    (3)   Sets - Seated-Overhead Presses

Day 3: (Back & Biceps)
    (3)   Sets - Pull Downs
    (3)   Sets - Barbell Curls

At times I have worked in specialty exercises such as grip and neck exercises.

As I mentioned earlier, I have a home gym so it is quite easy for me to conveniently take a short workout and stretch my routine over three (3) days. If you are a member of a gym and need to travel, or have only weekends available for weight training, here is an example of an effective one- day routine:

After a warm up, the following exercises are performed—two or three (2 or 3) sets of each:

- Squat
- Parallel Bar Dip or Bench Press
- Stiff-legged Dead-lift
- Dumbbell or Barbell Press
- Pull-down or Pull-up

- Barbell or Dumb Bell Curls
- Calf Work
- Abdominal Work

This is a full-body workout routine with which you can make great progress if you utilize it once a week. Needless to say, each exercise can be substituted for many other exercises that accomplish the same mission.

The foregoing was meant to be anything but a complete tutorial on weight training. My mission is to convince you of the importance of weight training for winning races and to offer some basic guidance to get you started. Read McRobert's book for detailed information that will have you shaping up in double time.

CHAPTER 17...

ENEMY OR FRIEND?

ALL ABOUT LACTIC ACID/THRESHOLD AND ENDURANCE TRAINING FOR YOUR BODY

One of the major goals in training is to build up the mitochondria in the muscles—the mechanism for utilizing and burning lactic acid efficiently and turning it into the energy you need to race.

The "pickups" and "speed drills" done the couple of days prior to an event—and as part of the warm up for the race—cause the release of enzymes that make the body more efficient in dissipating lactic acid. These enzymes are necessary to oxidize pyruvate which produces lactic acid in the body.

During your "hard training" sessions, you are building up the mitochondria in your muscles and increasing your lactic threshold (LT). In the final days prior to the event "pickups" keep the body on alert and releasing LA dissipating enzymes, but the hard work has really been done to make it your friend at race time.

One of the reasons I do my slow rides in between hammer fests is that it is the equivalent of long, slow distance (LSD) training in running, and is an incredibly efficient mechanism for slowly and effectively building more capillaries (small blood vessels)—called "capillarisation"—thereby making the transport of oxygen to working muscles much more efficient. Some people consider LSD as "garbage mileage." It is anything but, and has definite purpose(s).

After experiencing the lactic acid build up on your first couple of pick-up efforts, you will experience the feeling of having no lactic acid. That said, on the day before the race, I typically do about three (3) pick-ups which are intense enough to cause a feeling of lactic acid in my quadriceps, but not hard enough to cause any fatigue or feeling of having done much after recovery a few minutes later. I basically do the same thing at the end of my 25-35 mile spin two days prior to a race.

On race day, I do pickups during the last 15 minutes of my workout to where I am a bit breathless and definitely feel the lactic acid. By the time I get to the line, I typically feel like I can rip the cranks off the bike!

In a New York Times, nytimes.com article, 5/16/06, Gina Kolata, wrote: "Coaches and personal trainers tell athletes and exercisers that they have to learn to work out at just below their "lactic threshold," that point of diminishing returns when lactic acid starts to accumulate. Some athletes even have blood tests to find their personal lactic thresholds. But that, it turns out, is all wrong. Lactic acid is actually a fuel, not a caustic waste product. Muscles make it deliberately, producing it from glucose, and they burn it to obtain energy. The reason trained athletes can perform so hard and so long is because their intense training causes their muscles to adapt so they more readily and efficiently absorb lactic acid."

"Through trial and error, coaches learned that athletic performance improved when athletes worked on endurance, running longer and longer distances, for example. That, it turns out, increased the mass of their muscle mitochondria, letting them burn more lactic acid and allowing the muscles to work harder and longer."

Ms. Kolata quoted George A Brooks, a professor in the department of integrative biology at the University of California, Berkeley and Dr. L. Bruce Gladden, a professor of health and human performance at Auburn University who worked extensively and published his findings in the late 1970s which proved that lactic acid is in us for a reason and that is as a source of energy.

Training hard in brief spurts just before a race as Sandy coaches increases the mitochondria mass and is the reason for improved performance according to Dr. Brooks.

Improving Aerobic Capacity:

Given that high levels of lactate/hydrogen ions will be detrimental to performance, one of the key reasons for endurance training is to enable the body to perform at a greater pace with a minimal amount of lactate. This can be done by long, steady rides, which will develop the aerobic capacity by means of the capillarisation—enhancing oxygen transport to the muscles and by creating greater efficiency in the heart and lungs. If the aerobic capacity is greater, it means there will be more oxygen available to the working muscles and this should delay the onset of lactic acid at a given work intensity.

Improving Your Lactate Threshold:

The aim is to saturate the muscles with lactic acid in order to educate the body's buffering mechanism (alkaline) to deal with it more effectively. The accumulation of lactate in working skeletal muscles is associated with fatigue of this system after 50 to 60 seconds of maximal effort. Sessions should be comprised of one to five (1-5) repetitions (depends on the athlete's ability) with near to full recovery.

Training continuously at about 85% to 90% of your maximum heart rate for 20 to 25 minutes will improve your Lactate Threshold (LT). Once a week, commencing about 8 weeks before a major competition, you should begin this type of LT training. This will help the muscle cells retain their alkaline buffering ability. Improving your LT will also improve your VO2 max.

Most athletes see lactic acid as their enemy, and think that training helps them eliminate the metabolic waste product from their muscles so they will function longer and harder. But UC Berkeley physiologist George Brooks has found that training actually teaches your muscle cells how to use lactic acid as a fuel source to get more bang for the buck.

Training helps people get rid of the lactic acid before it can build to the point where it causes muscle fatigue, and at the cellular level, Brooks said, training means growing the mitochondria in muscle cells. The mitochondria, often called the "powerhouse of the cell," are where the lactate is burned for energy.

The world's best athletes stay competitive by interval training. The intense exercise generates big lactate loads and the body adapts by building up mitochondria to clear lactic acid quickly. If you use it up [as an energy source], it doesn't accumulate." ~ George A. Brooks, UC Berkley Professor of integrative biology (News Release)

I've included hard intervals in my training for years. What's different is that I now have a better understanding how my body uses lactic acid. My job is to challenge my body to handle more of it. Gradually increasing the intensity of my intervals seems to be the best way to do that.

Endurance training, in addition to interval training is vital to the success of your training. Cycling longer and longer distances, for example, increases the mass of an athlete's muscle mitochondria, letting them burn more lactic acid and allowing the muscles to work harder and longer.

CHAPTER 18...

THE KISS APPROACH TO HEART RATE ZONES

I'm a proponent of the KISS method of cycling training – there is no need to overcomplicate the process. David Heatley is an Australian cycling coach who offers coaching services and posts great information on cycling training/racing on his Cycling-Inform Website: www.cycling-inform.com Take the time to visit his wonderful site. Rather than do my own take on heart rate zones, the below information promulgated by David is not only well done, but follows the KISS approach. I got his permission to reproduce it rather than reinvent the wheel.

"If you do a search on heart rate zones, you'll get a large selection of zones with different values and number of zones—enough to get really confused. It seems that everyone has a different opinion on the matter. As we are regularly coaching cyclists that just want to get on and train right without having to get a degree in medical science, we keep our zones simple. I've found that these zones are very effective for the training required for cycling. They are slightly different to the ones that normally come as default with the Polar™ heart rate monitors. At the end of the day no one HR zone system is better than another. The important thing is to decide on one and then stick to it. In the table below and the descriptions that follow I describe the HR Zones that we use for our own personal training as well as the Remote Coaching program that we offer. This is one of the most effective ways of using your heart rate monitor to improve your cycling. "

DESCRIPTION	INTENSITY	CODE	ZONE
VO2 MAX Boosting	Very Hard – Can't speak	VO2	92 - 100%
Anaerobic Threshold Endurance	Hard – Difficult to speak at all	E3	85 - 91%
General Aerobic Endurance	Moderate – Talk in short sentences	E2	75 - 84%
Base Aerobic Endurance	Easy – Able to carry out conversation	E1	65 - 74%
Recovery	Easy – Able to carry out conversation	REC	50 - 64%

Cycling Australia Official Heart Rate Zones

Rest <50% MHR

This zone is associated with very light training and rest. Sometimes used during a transition phase in your training where you'll spend time walking or performing other very light cross training exercise. Sometimes referred to as "active recovery," this is the zone you generally use when you are stretching or performing other maintenance related activities like Pilates and yoga.

Zone REC (Recovery) 50 - 64% MHR

Sometimes combined with the next zone, this is a zone where you'll spend your time doing your recovery rides. It feels like you almost aren't training at all in this zone. It's a very important zone as it helps flush out your muscles in between intense training sessions. The key to this zone is to ensure that you don't go too hard because if you do you'll not be rested enough to go really hard in the harder session of your program.

Zone E1 (Aerobic Endurance) 65 - 74% MHR

This zone is where you build your aerobic base and is a zone that you'll spend a lot of time in when you are building your cycling base fitness. This zone is the foundation at the beginning of your season for which you'll build your strength then speed on throughout the year. This zone builds your aerobic power and enables you to ride long distances and improves your average speed while riding at an easy pace. This zone is normally associated with social riding. You are able to carry on a normal conversation, and is best done while riding with others at a relaxing pace. It's also the zone where you'll warm up and cool down.

Zone E2 (General Aerobic Endurance) 75-84%MHR

While this is an important zone for training to build an increase in muscle glycogen storage, you'll need to be careful spending time in this zone. It's sometimes referred to as "no-man's land" or "temp riding" as you are riding too fast to build your aerobic base but too slowly to develop your V02 MAX and lactate threshold. The result of spending too much time in this zone is that you'll get home feeling tired but not have really improved your fitness. Therefore this zone is not an efficient use of your training time. And… in a lot of cases it's the zone you'll be in when riding in medium paced bunch rides. For that reason it's important to monitor the time spent in this zone. In moderation, it is however a good zone to ease you into interval training and during a specialization period before starting to race. *Cyclists that train in this zone a lot end up quickly reaching a plateau in their fitness.*

Zone E3 (Anaerobic Threshold Endurance) 85-91%MHR

This zone is where you start to get some real improvements to your fitness. Referred to generally as "strength endurance training" this zone helps to increase your ability to ride at lactate threshold. It is a very important zone to train in for endurance events and road racing. This is not an easy zone to train in and is associated with interval training where you'll ride for short durations at an above average intensity. You'll be breathing hard in this zone and not able to carry on a conversation. Training in this zone helps build tolerance to the muscle burn that you get when riding hard as well as your strength endurance. *It's a critical zone to train in to be able to successfully bridge gaps, work in breaks, time trial and climb long hills.*

Zone VO2 (VO2 MAX Boosting) 92-100% MHR

Often referred to as "VO2MAX" this is the hardest zone to train in. This is a zone where you will increase your VO2MAX and build your heart's ability to increase its cardio output. It is mainly reserved for short and very intense intervals as it is not a zone that you can spend much time in. However, trained properly, cyclists can ride a short 20 minute individual time trial almost completely at the bottom of this zone. Holding a conversation is impossible. Use the lower end of this zone for very intense interval training and the higher end for sprint training."

From a personal perspective, my maximum heart rate is 193; hence my heart rate zone table would look as follows:

DESCRIPTION	INTENSITY	CODE	HEART RATE
VO2 MAX Boosting	Very Hard – Can't speak	VO2	177 - 193 BPM*
Anaerobic Threshold Endurance	Hard – Difficult to speak at all	E3	164 - 176 BPM*
General Aerobic Endurance	Moderate – Talk in short sentences	E2	144 - 163 BPM*
Base Aerobic Endurance	Easy – Able to carry out conversation	E1	121 - 143 BPM*
Recovery	Easy – Able to carry out conversation	REC	96 - 120 BPM*

** BPM - Beats Per Minute*

A heart rate monitor is a very valuable training tool and I suggest that you build your own table once you determine your maximum heart rate.

The only time I am in the VO2 zone is when I am sprinting or racing rather hard to close a gap in a fast group ride or race. I have found through meticulous record keeping and experimentation that I time trial best in the upper regions of E3 zone – this means an average heart rate of around 172-173 when I am racing well. Usually when I road race, I average in the lower to mid regions of E3 – typically 165-171. During fast group rides, I typically average in the mid E2 to the low end of E3.

Interestingly, during a hard interval session of repeat ½ mile work intervals at 5-10% above my planned time trial speed, I will often have an average heart rate of 145-150 for a workout of six (6) intervals including the time between intervals as I reposition for the next – typically about a 12 minute workout. My peak heart rate for the workout typically falls somewhere within the E3 zone.

During the time of the year that I am not racing or peaking for an event, I do most of my riding in the REC-E1 zones. Typically when I ride home from a group ride, I do so in the rest zone which for me is a heart rate below 96. I often pull into my driveway after a 70 mile ride with a heart rate in the 70s to low 80s.

Keep in mind that heart rate is very much affected by many variables such as the amount of rest prior to the workout, temperature, humidity, etc. Although I use a heart rate monitor for workouts and training, the best, albeit expensive approach to training, is, ideally, with a power meter. Most masters riders I know simply use a heart rate monitor, which as you can see is a very effective tool.

I determined my maximum heart rate in the field. In the past two years racing in our state road race championships in temperatures of over 100 degrees and then sprinting at the end of each race with every bit of effort that I could muster from my body, I hit a maximum heart rate both years of 193.

The following information provided by Coach David Heatley offers some methods for determining your maximum heart rate.

"It is a question that I get asked a lot. The following article provides methods for testing for your MAX Heart Rate (MAX HR). Knowing your MAX HR will enable you to work out your heart rate zones."

"The 220 minus age formula that was developed in the Second World War to work out your max heart rate is rather dated but still used extensively around the world. A new formula '214-(0.8 x age) for men, and 209-(0.9 x age) for women' has been developed to help improve its accuracy."

"Quoting:
http://www.runnersworld.co.uk/news/article.asp?uan=181"

'The traditional strategy is to use the formula of 220 minus age to 'guesstimate your max'. This is often used in health clubs. Here, charts show age-related MHR and training heart rates for cardiovascular fitness development. For example, if you are 40, your estimated MHR would be 180 (i.e. 220-40). You can then calculate training heart rates from this, using a formula such as 70 per cent MHR (which would be 126). It's quite simple, but unfortunately it's not accurate for everyone. American sports scientists have modified the basic formula to allow for gender: 214-(0.8 x age) for men, and 209-(0.9 x age) for women.'"

"Both the '220 minus age' and '214-(0.8 x age)' for men, and '209-(0.9 x age)' for women' formulas will provide you with a good starting point however, most people that I train have a higher max heart rate than these normalized formulas."

"For a more accurate indication of your personal max heart rate there are several simple cycling max heart rate tests that you can perform yourself or with the aid of someone else."

"The following methods are sourced from http://www.timetrialtraining.co.uk/S6MaxHeartRateTests.htm and provide two good examples of max heart rate tests:"

Max Heart Rate - Test 1

'This test requires a Heart Rate Monitor and a turbo trainer. It may be helpful to have someone assist during the test, to encourage you when things get tough and to take the readings from your Heart Rate Monitor.

- *Warm up for 10 to 15 minutes and then Ride as hard as possible —intensive Time Trial effort—for the next ten minutes. Ride the last minute flat out (maximum effort), and sprint the last 20 to 30 seconds. It should now be possible to read the MHR on the Heart Rate Monitor.*
- *Do not stop immediately but keep pedaling and warm down gradually for the next ten minutes.*
- *Repeat the test two or three more times, with a couple of days between each test, to establish your true maximum."*

Max Heart Rate - Test 2

"This test requires a Heart Rate Monitor, turbo trainer and a computer (ideally with a cadence measurement). Your bicycle should have a close ratio rear block (e.g. 52 x 18/17/16/15/14/13). Have someone assist during the test, to encourage you when things get tough and to take the readings from your Heart Rate Monitor.

- *Warm up fully for 10 to 15 minutes.*
- *Use your large chain ring and choose the lowest gear (e.g. 52 x 18). Pedal at a steady cadence of 90 rpm for 2 minutes.*
- *Then change up to the next gear (52 x 17) without pausing.*
- *Maintain the same cadence (90-rpm). Pedal this gear for 2 minutes and change up again still maintaining the 90-rpm cadence.*
- *Continue changing up to the next sprocket every two minutes, constantly maintaining 90-rpm.*
- *Your heart rate should rise constantly. It may level out at some point (your OHR) but carry on with the test.*
- *Continue at 90 rpm, changing up a sprocket every two minutes, until you are no longer able to go on.*
- *Do not stop immediately but keep pedaling and warm down gradually for the next ten minutes."*

"I personally prefer a variation on Max Heart Rate -Test 1; performed on a short 500m hill which ends in a sharp gradient towards the top.

- *Warm up for 10-15 minutes riding into the E3 Heart Rate Zone*
- *Ride up the hill as fast as you can then sprint up the last section.*
- *Recover and repeat a few times.*
- *Record your Max Heart Rate for each effort and take the highest reading.*
- *Cool down for ten to fifteen minutes."*

"It's important to perform this a few times in one session as you may need to fatigue a little to reach your maximum heart rate (MHR)."

"Another way, if you are racing, is to check for your maximum heart rate data on a regular basis. You will usually reach your maximum heart rate during the final sprint finish of most races where you end up sprinting at 100%."

CHAPTER 19...

METHODS FOR TESTING YOUR FITNESS

Recovery Pulse Index and Basal Pulse Rate

Part of training is always knowing where you are physically. Some athletes rely on biorhythms or "just how" they feel. A much more accurate way to gauge where your body is on any given day of training is through the monitoring of your RPI and BPR rates.

Recovery Pulse Index (RPI)

A quick method to check your fitness improvement is through establishing a Base One Level and occasional testing of your Recovery Pulse Index (RPI).

Basically, your RPI is how much your heart slows down in one (1) minute after five (5) minutes of intense exercise. The quicker your recovery, the stronger or more effective your heart is.

The best way of accomplishing this test is through use of a heart rate monitor such as the many models offered by Polar.

- Exercise very hard - ideally as hard as you can - for five (5) minutes and note your heart rate at the end of the five (5) minutes.
- Exactly one (1) minute later, check your heart rate again. Your RPI number is the difference between the two figures.

A person in excellent condition will have an RPI of 30 beats or higher—use the higher difference between the two numbers--on the second reading.

If you do not have a heart rate monitor, take your pulse on the side of your neck or your wrist for six (6) seconds and multiply by 10.

The reason for taking your pulse for such a brief period is the fact that your heart rate typically will be coming down quite rapidly. Obviously, the most accurate reading would be use of a heart rate monitor. I recommend establishing a base rate and periodically checking to see how you are progressing.

Basal Pulse Rate:

As you have undoubtedly noticed as you have become fitter, your resting pulse rate goes down. Athletes involved in aerobic sports will often have resting pulse rates in the forties. I once had a training partner whose resting pulse was in the thirties.

Basically, your **Basal Pulse Rate (BPR)** is your pulse when you first awaken in the morning. My preferred method for checking BPR is:

- Upon awakening and using the bathroom, return to bed and lie down for at least a couple of minutes.
- Then check your pulse rate by measuring it for one (1) minute. Assuming that the previous day did not include a particularly stressful workout, that is your basal pulse rate.

My BPR is almost always around 46 - it has been as low as 42 after a complete day off the previous day. If you notice that your BPR has increased about 10% one morning, you probably should not plan intervals or a hard ride that day, but either rest or do a recovery ride. As you can see BPR is both a measure of fitness and a measure of overtraining, and hence an interesting, useful tool.

CHAPTER 20...

THE MOMENT OF TRUTH
THE ART OF RACING A TIME TRIAL

"Cycling, to me, isn't a sport, it isn't a hobby, and it isn't an interest. Cycling, to me, is a passion and where passion comes from, there is no pain, there is no suffering, but only the love of pain and suffering. And a passion is something you never quit, you never forget, and something you will always love. A passion is forever, cycling is forever. **"Coryn Rivera, 16 years old; 23-times National Junior Cycling Champion**

The grit of this 16 year old is amazing to me. She is competing against cyclists years older and winning all of her races. I am also extremely passionate about my cycling and believe that you must have a deep passion to win time trial races because, if you are, you will put your entire heart and soul—and your guts into the race and get to the finish line as the winner. So, if you have the heart and passion for it, what I have to say in this chapter will help you get the gold medals.

WARNING: The information you are about to read will make you a faster time trial racer. If you are a cyclist who likes to race simply to participate, and if you enjoy paying money to race with no hope of winning, or if racing is just a social event for you, this chapter may or may not be of interest to you. Prior to giving up on the chapter however, please read at least the paragraph for a different perspective by Dave Viney, and world-class time trial competitor.

If, however, you are a hard core racer or want to be one with all your heart and you go to the race to win, then you believe as I do: that the only winner in a race is the guy on the top step of the podium and the other two guys on the podium are the first and second losers. This information is vital to your winning races.

Dave Viney is the finest time trial rider I have ever known. He is a multiple gold-medal winner in the Canadian National Masters Time Trial championships as well as multiple-event winner in the North American Masters Time Trial championships. He rode the fastest times in those meet for anyone over 30 while he was in his 50s!

Dave is currently 59 years old, and, in most time trial events, he turns in the top time overall beating even the Pro, One, and Two racing groups. A month before his planned-peak form for the Canadian and North American Masters championships, Dave rode a 40 kilometer time trial at the United States Cycling Federation's Florida State Time Trial Championships in 52:55 at the age of 58 – that's an incredible 28.2 mph average for almost 25 miles!

Having the utmost respect for Dave and knowing that his training is "the best", I asked him to comment on my time trial racing chapter. He is very straight forward: *"Not to quibble but I kind of like the TT because you are competing against yourself so everyone can be a "winner" by improving on previous performances on the same course hence the popularity of the thousands of weekly club-run TT's."*

In that Dave is my time trial hero, our differing philosophical outlook notwithstanding, in deference to him, I invite those of you who are casual racers to read on. You will find other comments by Dave italicized throughout this chapter.

Time trialing is called the "Race of Truth" for good reason. There are no wheels to suck, and there are no excuses – you are on your own, you are in the wind, and there is no place to hide! If you listen to the chatter at the end of the typical road race, you will hear many of the following statements: "I got boxed in," "I didn't know someone was off the front," "I was driven wide in the last turn," "Someone sat up in front of me," "My lead out man went too early," "My lead out man went too late," etc., etc., etc.. There are no excuses in a time trial – you either cover the distance faster than everyone else or you lose.

There is admittedly an element of luck, and certainly a lot of strategy in road racing and, hence, the strongest rider does not necessarily win. In time trial races, assuming equal equipment, preparation, technique, and the ability and willingness to experience pain, the strongest rider will almost always win. I love that! *"In a TT the strongest rider who does the best job at pacing and maximizing his effort, and who has done his homework in equipment preparation and course review, will win."*

To be an outstanding time trial racer, you need not only a strong engine, but you must be willing and able to withstand rather intense pain. To me, that kind of pain is "delightful pain" – I embrace it! You must also be able to concentrate. Otherwise, if you let your mind wander, you will assuredly allow your speed or power to fall off leading to a result below your potential. Time trial riding is hard work and you have a lot of tasks in addition to just riding your bike fast!

While on the subject of pain, I have never forgotten a statement made by Olympic swimming champion, Don Schollander, who set three world records en route to winning four (4) gold medals at the 1964 Olympics. When asked by a reporter what separates a champion from the rest of the pack he said, *"The difference between a champion and a non-champion is, that when the body is screaming out in pain, the champion pushes his body even harder while the others do not."*

If you are still reading this, let's deal with specifics. I will assume that you are serious enough about time trial racing that you have equipped yourself properly with the basic necessities for an optimal performance:

1. You have a dedicated time trial bicycle with aero wheels that has been properly fitted to you.

2. You plan to wear a skin suit, aerodynamic helmet, booties over your shoes, and no gloves.

3. You will run with a water bottle on the seat tube if you have a bicycle with round tubing.

Race Preparation:

It is the day before a time trial race at which you plan to compete. I suggest that you prepare a checklist of the things you wish to bring with you that can be printed out and used every time you go to an event. With both of us racing, Rosie put together a spreadsheet of all of the things we need to take with us. It is easy to forget things in the hustle to get out the door with so much stuff—especially with two of us racing. Check off each item prior to leaving home so you have no surprises the next morning.

Some of the things that I bring in addition to the obvious are:

- Extra wheels so that I don't need to struggle with tire/wheel issues when I should be warming up or thinking about the race.

- Spray adhesive (recommended by Dr. Joe Branconi, a super time trial racer, at my first competition). I use Duro All-Purpose Adhesive™ or Elmer's Craft Bond™ spray adhesives for affixing the racing number to my jersey. Numbers that are pinned tend to flap in the breeze which is distracting and not aerodynamic— and they also hard to put on with pins and can put holes and pulls into your very expensive skin suit.

- A tool kit with everything I might need for minor repairs including vinyl gloves.

- A tire pump.

- A bike stand on which to prop your bicycle.

- Essentials: Pre-race meal items and energy gel(s) and bars, sun block, water and other fluids, etc. If you like a banana in the morning, don't plan on getting one at your hotel at 5:30 a.m.

Clean your bike thoroughly – "a clean bike is a fast bike"—as told by his Dad to Mike McCollum, a 50-year-veteran of the racing circuit, Olympic Games alternate, and a national cycling Coach of the Year.

Check your tires carefully for any chards of glass or anything else that might later cause a flat. Inflate your tires prior to leaving home. You don't need the surprise and aggravation of a presta valve failure or any other tire issues the morning of the race. *"I vary pressures depending on road surface- 150-160 psi for a hard, smooth surface, down to 120 on a chip-and- seal-type surface."* Although this is probably stating the obvious, do not run 150 pounds of pressure in a tire designed for a maximum of 125 pounds! I use tubular tires which typically have much higher inflation limits than clinchers.

If the race is the next morning and far enough from your home to require a hotel stay, arrive during daylight hours to leave yourself enough time to go out to the race course and familiarize yourself with it and the time it will take to get there in the morning.

Drive or ride the course noting turns, landmarks, condition of the road, hazards, etc. I'm a firm believer in the process of visualization prior to an athletic event. With the course in mind, you can envision yourself successfully racing the course.

However, do not be surprised if you find that the course has not been marked and that there are creatures in the middle of the road on your arrival. At one time trial event, while driving the course the afternoon prior to the race, we found three bulls wandering around the road. Not cows – actual bulls!! Somehow, according to our experiences, it does get taken care of in the morning by the race director or volunteers. However, if you do see glass, sand, and other hazards when you are out riding the course, mention them to the race director in the morning to insure that they have been marked. Nothing is worst than being in the zone and hitting sand going around a corner.

Try to get a good night's sleep the night before the race, but, if you find yourself nervous and unable to readily sleep, remember that the two nights previous to that night are the important nights to sleep well.

Arise early enough to allow at least three (3) hours between your pre-race meal and the actual race. Eat a very light pre-race meal – even a light feeding will feel like a five (5) course dinner on a nervous stomach, but a light meal will be digested by race time. Experiment with your pre-race meal to see what works best for you. Even though I drink a glass of orange juice every morning prior to my workout, I don't do well with it on a nervous, pre-race stomach.

Through experimentation, my pre-race meal has evolved to the following: A Clio™ bar, banana, and water to drink. As a competitive runner, I got into the habit of taking two pre-race aspirins as both a blood thinner (controversial) and to mask the various aches and pains that I seemed to chronically suffer while pursuing that sport. I have continued the habit with my cycling races, and, if nothing else, I benefit from the placebo effect in the belief that my performance will be enhanced and my neck will not hurt!

Out of curiosity, I contacted a physician friend of mine who happens to also be an avid time trial competitor to get his perspective on the use of aspirins pre-competition. He, told me that commencing at the age of 50, he began a regimen of taking a daily low dose aspirin of 81 mg. On race day, he ups his dose to two 350 mg aspirins "as a heart attack/stroke preventative." *Each of us is unique; you have to experiment and find out what works for you. For some people a little caffeine (coffee, coke, or tablet) helps with especially short TT's early in the day.*

Many times, trial events will post start times either on the Internet or at the official, event hotel the night prior to the race. If possible, ascertain your start time the night before the race, and pick up your race packet if available. Place your number on your skin suit that night. It saves valuable time and effort in the morning when you need to concentrate on the race and warming up.

If you do not have a start time and/or race packet in advance, plan to arrive at the race venue at least one and one-half hours prior to the start time of the first racer. Register immediately and affix your race number to your skin suit. If transponders are being used for timing, install it or have it installed on your bike.

Check your start time, and sync your watch with the official race clock. Cruise by the start periodically to see that they are keeping to a published schedule - your time starts when they say "GO" for your number regardless of whether you are there or not – there is NO excuse for missing your start time—although I have had Rosie screaming at me and waving me on near the start line as the starter is looking for me. I like to keep warming up until the very last minute.

Prior to commencing your warm-up, check your bicycle for any obvious issues. Make sure that your wheels are spinning freely, your computer is working, and that your brake pad is not pressing against a wheel from lying in your car. Plan to warm up for at least an hour for a time trial event. Every time trial requires a very warm engine at the start so that you can achieve your goal pace immediately without feeling either physical or nervous system distress.

The first half-hour of your warm up should be comprised of easy spinning. In the second half hour you should commence doing race-pace pickups allowing some lactic acid to build up and dissipate. Finally, finish your workout with a couple of brief sprints. Your legs and system will be ready for battle. Some competitors use trainers for their warm-up. Ideally, I warm up on the race course as I would rather feel the road as I will experience it in the race. Dave Viney's warm-up routine is as follows:

"I warm-up for the first 45 min. or so on my road bike - more comfortable, less worry about punctures, got spare with me in case etc, then for last 45 min. move to TT bike and TT helmet, booties etc. and do several hard efforts getting up to race wattage for extended periods-3-5 min.- I have found that doing a warm-up on a trainer was not good for me - I have to feel the road and the power of the wind and how it will affect me in TT position- I've got to get comfortable with wind buffeting me and how bike will handle at 30mph in that wind on that road. The shorter the TT the longer and harder the warm up – ambient temperature also needs to be considered but maybe that is a whole other article."

It is 10 minutes prior to your start time….

The race begins. You have completed a thorough warm-up, and it is 10 minutes until your start time. Earlier, you had checked to make sure that the start times were going as scheduled.

Prior to getting to your place in line, put your bicycle in the gear with which you will start the race. I typically start in 53-14, assuming no wind and a flat roadway at the starting line. (Note: Gear "53" is the big chain ring and "14" is the fourth (4th) cog over from the right on my time trial bike which is equipped with an 11/23 cassette. Shimano Dura-ace gruppos come with a gear indicator installed on the right shifter for readily determining the gear that you are currently using without looking down.

If you start in too low a gear, you will spin out too quickly leading to unnecessary, early shifting. If you start in too high a gear, your legs will be forced to make a harder effort than needed to efficiently get off the line. You need to try this in practice to find your own best starting gear and then consider start conditions. Some of the variables include an up or down slope, tailwind, fast, sharp turn just off the line, ramp start, holder or foot-down start.

I have had the experience of my chain coming off while being held for the start and pedaling backwards to position my cranks to clip in with my second foot. Because bar-end shifters are constantly variable, it is easy to not be precisely in gear with them. Upon completion of shifting into your starting gear, roll your cranks backwards for a few repetitions to assure yourself that the chain will not come off at the starting line.

There is a tendency for competitors to line up for a time trial much too early – a time that would be better spent completing a thorough warm-up. You will find many of them casually chatting as they await their turn to start. You, on the other hand, will take your starting place just minutes before your scheduled start. Your engine will be well warmed up, and you will be ready to immediately commence a hard effort without shocking your body and getting needless lactic acid buildup. You will have time to chat when you collect your gold medal.

Ready, Set, Go!

It is usual for the racers to start in either one- minute or 30-second intervals and be lined up by number. When you are number one in line or set to go next, pull your bike up to the starting line, clip in with one foot, apply your brake(s), and confirm with your holder that he or she has you securely held prior to clipping in with your second foot. Some competitors do not feel comfortable being clipped in and balanced by a holder. If you do not wish to be held, inform the starters of that fact as you pull up to the start position.

Note: Rosie preferred being held long before I trusted someone enough and recognized that it gave me a better start in that you are in your pedals and set to put the power-to-the-pedal immediately at the end of countdown. The major downside to not being held is that, sometimes with the adrenalin flowing, it can be difficult to clip into the other pedal when you are released.

Place the pedal of your power leg at the 2:00 o'clock or 10:00 o'clock position in preparation for coming off the line with a powerful down stroke. Reset your computer to zero so you have an independent measure of your time and accurate distance. You don't want to be manipulating anything but your pedals when you are given the "go" signal. If you are using a heart-rate monitor, start it with five (5) seconds to go in the countdown, and get out of the seat in preparation for the release by your holder.

When the starter finishes your countdown, accelerate very briskly to get up to race pace. A fast start is particularly important in a short time trial such as one contested over 5K. Remember, often fractions of a second separate the finishers and you don't want to lose the race due to poor start.

As an aside, a study of running milers showed that coming off the line very fast in the first 10 seconds led to no more of an anaerobic state than coming off the line slower. The same holds true for a cycling start. Let's assume that your planned average speed for a 5K race is 25 mph. Remember, you are not only starting from zero, but most time trial races have a 180 degree turn at the half-way point where you can lose most of your momentum. This means that when you are looking at your computer, you had better be looking at more than 25 mph in order to achieve your planned average.

Continue your acceleration as you look down the road, and, when you have reached your race pace, settle back onto your seat and your aero bars. Often times, your adrenalin will carry you to speeds much too fast to sustain. I, for example, am often surprised when I first check my computer to discover that I am doing over 30 mph. Slowly let your speed bleed off to your planned race pace. Understand that speed can be VERY misleading in that there might be a head or tail wind and/or down- or up-slope. For those of you who use power meters, wattage is the ultimate gauge of effort.

There are many conflicting philosophies and techniques as to how to properly race a time trial. Some coaches advise to treat the first-half of the race as if it were the whole race, and then use everything that you have left to race the second half. I don't always agree with this. Assuming no wind, I have found that I can achieve the best times by racing a negative split; i.e., racing the second half of the race faster than the first half. The danger with the opposite strategy is blowing up prior to the finish.

My philosophy of racing on windy days is a bit different. Many racers are quite conservative when the starting leg is into the wind. They try to conserve energy reasoning that they will make it up by going very fast on the downwind leg. In these conditions, especially in a short race like the commonly-contested 5K at Senior Games events, I treat the headwind portion of the race as if the turnaround point is the finish line. I know through experience that once I turn around, I will be able to still go fast on the downwind leg. Using that technique at the 2007 Florida State Senior Games, I was able to break both the 5K and 10K state records on a day in which there was a very brisk headwind on the outbound leg, and many racers performed well below their potential.

I believe in putting extra effort into the slowest part of the course where, for example, there are headwinds, hills, etc. This is where you spend and gain the most time. You might be saying to yourself, "Great theory pal, but it just doesn't make sense to me." As a retired airline pilot whose degree is in engineering, let me demonstrate my thesis using an airplane and a simple mathematical problem:

Assume that a 100 mile east/west (200 mile total) course has been marked out in the sky. Assume that there is no wind. An airplane flying at 100 mph enters the course flying in an easterly direction, traverses the course, makes a 180 degree turn, re-enters the course and flies the course in a westerly direction.

According to the formula of D=RT (distance equals rate of speed multiplied by time), solving the equation for T (time) reveals that the airplane took a total of 2 hours flying the 200 mile round trip. Note that we are only counting the time on the course. Now, assume that the wind conditions change, and there is a 10 mph wind from the east. The airplane again enters the course flying at an indicated speed of 100 mph, and flies the eastbound section of the course with a 10 mph headwind (groundspeed would be 90 mph). The aircraft reverses direction now flying the westerly portion of the course with a 10 mph tailwind (groundspeed would be 110 mph). The question is, did it: (A) Take the same amount of time in both examples to fly the round trip? Or (B) Less time with the wind added? Or (C) More time when the wind was added?

The answer is not as important as the reason for the answer. The answer is "C": It takes longer to fly the course when the wind becomes a factor. The reason for that result is that the aircraft spends more time flying at a slower ground speed in the headwind than it does when it is flying faster due to the tailwind of equal intensity. In other words, you are flying for a longer period of time while being bogged down by the headwind than you are when being helped by the tailwind. Hence, the headwind has more of a negative effect than the tailwind has a positive effect.

There is no way of making that time up unless speed is increased. If you do not expend an extra effort in the headwind, the same phenomenon will be the cause of you riding a slower time trial. Admittedly, it is a painful, albeit effective, technique!

So, there you are racing the course: You have settled into your aero-position, you are riding at your planned race pace (or power goal), and the pain is getting a bit uncomfortable. What often separates the winners from the losers is mental attitude and work. The poor time trial rider often deals with the pain by disassociation – the rider thinks of pleasant, distracting things to get his or her mind off of the incessant pain. The good time trial rider embraces the pain, and works at testing the limits of that pain. You don't have to slow down simply because you are experiencing lactic acid build up in your legs. Perhaps you can even increase your speed without suffering additional pain. And if you do suffer additional pain, embrace it!

You must constantly be aware of your effort, speed (and/or power when using a power meter) and focus on the race. It is vital that you constantly run checks on your position and your body. Make sure that your speed has not slowed ever so slightly and, if it has, you must increase your effort to regain your planned pace (or power). Check that your body is relaxed and that you do not have a "death grip" on the bars and your head is not tucked into your shoulders. Remember, you have a fuel tank with a finite amount of fuel to use in the race. The ideal expenditure of fuel is to empty the tank as you cross the finish line.

Excessive gripping of the bar, grimacing of the face, tightness in the shoulders, etc., all use fuel unnecessarily. Check your knee position – they should be very close to the top tube in your pedal stroke. The more you let your knees wander from the optimal position, the less efficiently you will be able to cut through the air. Check your shoulder position – make sure you are not bringing them up towards your ears. Push your abdomen towards the top tube to be more aerodynamic. You must constantly monitor these things throughout the duration of the race. Be sure you are belly breathing rather than inefficient and enervating chest breathing. Relax!

If the race is a technical course, be aware of your surroundings. I personally seem to lose a lot of my cognitive skills when I am performing at a maximal effort. As an example, at the Senior Olympics in 2007, I was sure that I was en route to a winning effort based on my pace and the closure with other racers well known to me. I rounded a turn at about 30 mph, turned down a steep roadway only to be confronted by barricades at the end. I had gone off course! I had to make a 180 degree turn, climb a steep grade only to arrive 30 seconds later at a spot that I had been doing 30 mph rather than almost zero.

Needless to say, I lost that important race. Last year at our USCF state road race championships, I was the lead cyclist following a police motorcycle escort. I was so intense and focused on racing fast that, when the motorcycle made a 90-degree right turn on the actual course, I kept going straight and off course. I fortunately caught up and won the race. Going off course happens, and, when it does, it is embarrassing and you have wasted all of your preparation time by making a simple mistake. It is hard to blow it off when you are in a major event that should have been won—I know first hand!

Now you are approaching the turnaround and, hopefully, you went around it a couple of times before the race and feel comfortable rounding it. As you are approaching the turnaround point, *slow down before the turn;* and, as you go around the first cone, you should be slightly heading to your right so that you are at somewhat of an angle; you are heading out of the turn and as you pass the cone, you are heading straight down the road and you should get out of your saddle and up on your pedals and accelerate back to race-pace prior to settling back into your aero position.

It is particularly vital to make an efficient, SAFE (I have fractured my neck in a turn on a time trial course) turn in a short time trial. As an aside, practicing turns as part of your training will be time well spent. The barriers in the turn, officials, and cones can be quite intimidating and distracting so practice a few times on the course by rounding them before the race.

When you practice your turns, try to simulate race conditions by approaching at race pace, not braking too soon, and losing as little momentum as possible in the turn. This will also give you an opportunity to choose your optimal braking point for the race. It is not unusual for riders to come out of one of their pedals as they are going around the turn, thinking that they are not going to make it. It causes a racer to lose a lot of time and energy getting back into the cleat and onto the aero bars. Of all the things that can cause you to lose seconds and the race, coming out of your pedal is the thing most likely to do so.

Focus on riders that started before you – try to close on them. A successful technique that some use to close in on the competition is focusing on a road sign or other landmark and making believe that it is a strong magnet pulling you towards it.

Continue to check your pace, position on the bike, hands, face and shoulders for relaxation. As you tire, there is a tendency to mash down on the pedals. Check your pedal stroke for smoothness and symmetry. By now, you are probably seriously hurting, but allow yourself a brief moment away from the business at hand to envision that championship medal and jersey that you are about to win.

Last year at the Florida State USCF time trial championships contested at 20K for my age group, the second half of the race was into the wind. The pain was so intense that I promised my body that if it let me not blow up and win the State championship, I would never subject it to that kind of punishment again! It did, but, of course, I broke my promise!

Here is what Dave Viney is thinking towards the end of a time trial effort: *"Over the last few km I keep repeating the mantra –' I am not going to lose this damn race by a few seconds after all this pain –keep the pressure on –don't put yourself in the position to be saying: 'If I had known he was 3 seconds ahead of me I could have caught him but I didn't know' - just assume somebody out there is within a sec. of you so every second does matter - don't give it away at the end!"*

As they get tired, many racers make the mistake of dropping their neck and looking down at the road. If you are wearing an aero helmet and you do that, it simply places a big wind catcher (the long pointed end of the helmet) into the airstream. Maintain your position on the bike. Many riders make the mistake of continuously searching for a gear that "feels better." Find that gear that enables you to run at a very efficient time trial cadence of around 85-95 rpm, and stick with it!

At last, the finish line is in sight! You have nothing different to do than you have been doing. If you are able to speed up or sprint at this point, you have not held a fast enough pace. You should have nothing left in your tank as you approach the finish line which means you were running on fumes.

As you can see, there are a lot of things to consider and think about in order to ride an efficient, fast time trial. You have no time to spare to disassociate yourself from the task at hand. If you have practiced the above techniques in your interval training, they will become second nature when you race. You race as you train.

Do a nice warm down on your bicycle, and ideally arrive at the awards ceremony in time to take your place on the top step of the podium.

If you are competing in the typical Senior Games events, there will be both 5K & 10K time trials. Continue to ride your bike between the events to keep your legs loose. I consume an athletic gel such as Clif Shots™ between races, hydrate myself, and start thinking about the next race. If you put forth the maximum effort that you should have in the first race, you might entertain thoughts of scratching from the second race. Don't do it! You will find as you warm down that you will finally stop feeling like you are sick to your stomach and your lungs are on fire as many often do at the end of a hard-run time trial – especially an early season effort—and often you can get a better time on the 10K race.

Train, plan, and race hard, and enjoy one of the most self-satisfying experiences in our sport – a well ridden, gold-medal-winning time trial race!

CHAPTER 21...

ROAD RACING

Victory belongs to an antagonist who knows how to suffer one quarter of an hour longer. Marcel Proust

Marcel Proust, the novelist, must have had road racing in mind when he made that statement. Unlike time trial racing, my favorite form of cycling competition, road racing is basically a team sport. On the professional level, most teams have a leader and a rider whose specialty is sprinting.

During multiple day races, called stage races, there are usually multiple objectives other than just finishing at the top of the leader board—or "general classification" as it is called. For example, in The Tour de France, teams are vying for not only the coveted yellow jersey which goes to the rider who has the lowest cumulative elapsed time, but other jerseys also awarded daily: The green jersey is awarded to the rider accumulating the most sprinter points; the polka dot jersey is awarded to the best climber, and the white jersey is awarded to the best young rider under 25; there is even a daily prize for the most aggressive rider. Vying for these prized jerseys involves rather complicated strategies and quickly changing tactics.

The teams are constantly in radio contact with the team director who follows the racers in the team car. The director feeds race information to the team members and typically dictates the tactics. Finally at the end of the race, the winner receives the yellow jersey, and the winners of the other competitions receive appropriate jerseys.

During flat stages, the strategy revolves around getting the team's sprinter in a position such that he can be led out to a winning performance by his teammates who typically form a train, peeling off one by one, and finally leaving the sprinter to do his thing at the end, fighting it out with the other sprinters. On the other stages, the goal of the team is to protect the leader, allowing him to rest as much as possible in the draft of team members, and ultimately win the race and be atop the general classification at the end.

Sometimes at the start of the race, even the team is unclear as to who its leader is. Probably the best example is the 2009 Tour de France. At the start of the race, it was unclear whether Alberto Contador, the 2007 winner of the tour, or Lance Armstrong, who won seven (7) Tours de France races in a row would be the leader. It did not sort itself out until Contador showed himself to be the strongest rider on the team in the first big mountain stage.

Road racing is rather complicated, and I consider it to be a chess game on wheels. The strongest rider often does not win as is the case with a time trial race. My training partner whom you met earlier in the book, Mike McCollum, opines that it takes about five (5) years to learn the art of road racing.

On an amateur level, road racing is still a team sport, but typically not as organized as professional racing. There will be various tactics employed such as blocking for a team member who might be off the front of the peloton, but typically due to the wide discrepancy in talent of the team members, tactics are not as readily and successfully deployed on other than the top teams.

Typically, as the age group level increases there is less of an impact made by teams, and the team phenomenon is virtually non existent in age groups such as the 60+ group. In Senior Games racing as opposed to USCF events, team racing is all but non existent.

However, every day we masters are on a club ride and in a group, we are giving everything we have to stay with the group in front and have enough energy to win at least one of the sprints or getting the satisfaction of doing long, fast pulls. If nothing else, just not getting dropped, and being with the front pack at the end. There is no "official leader", but there are those like Sandy who will lead out a ride and maintain a pace of 20 mph for all of the riders in the group and insure that no one gets left behind. Then, the next day, he is tearing up the road and leading out a ride to Pass-a-Grille—a beautiful county park at the end of the barrier islands of St. Petersburg and closest point to the Sunshine Skyway Bridge--at 26-30 mph and having a great time of it. He is the State of Florida Senior Games and USCF age group champion road racer over 65 years. He puts in a lot of hours on the bike to insure that he is a winner—every day.

Most venues which offer cycling as a Senior Games' sport, only have five 5K & 10K time trial events which are much easier to manage than 20K & 40K road races – the distances contested in Senior Games competitions. Even in the State of Florida where there are numerous races from September to April, the number of cities and/or counties sponsoring road races has dwindled over the past several years. It is becoming increasingly difficult for Senior Games' cyclists to find a venue in which to qualify for the championships.

If you choose to contest USCF sanctioned road races, you will find that the oldest age group offered is the Masters 55+ group. Unfortunately, cycling has not evolved to the point of running competitions which have offered five-year age groups as far back as I can remember. Fortunately, the USCF does offer five-year age groups typically for state and certainly for national championships.

If you decide to participate in a road race, one thing it has in common with a time trial race is the need for a sufficient warm-up. A warm-up of approximately one (1) hour for road races is almost a guarantee for a good start. It is best to use basically the same warm up given in the chapter on time trial racing.

The importance of a thorough warm-up is to be able to cover an early break-away attempt. If you are not sufficiently warmed up, you might find yourself not ready to efficiently cover a fast start and end up in an unfavorable position for the rest of the race. You will, however, find many road races that seem to be slower than your local group rides.

I, Sandy, have participated in road races where I literally talked with a fellow competitor for virtually the complete distance. However, I have also been in events where I suffered as much as I do in a time trial, and have maxed-out my heart rate well into the 190-plus region.

My favorite tactic, being a reasonably good time trial rider, is to get into a small breakaway group, and then, ultimately, do a single breakaway from that group. That tactic has garnered me three (3) state road race championships. My favorite time to try for a breakaway is just after the person I perceive to be my main competition finishes a pull. That is a great time to attack unexpectedly and hard!

You will find that road racing seems to bring out the latent police officer in a few people. I call them "The Peloton Police." They will tell you how to ride, where to go, and if you don't comply with their wishes, many can get loud and abusive. I used to have a reputation of taking the ride out on the road a lot faster than most people were capable of doing—and I got yelled at!

Do not pay any attention to those folks who are trying to control you in a race. You must race your own race, and let them race theirs. You are not racing to win a popularity contest – your goal is to make it to the top step of the podium. I find it rather maddening when I am doing a lot of the work in a road race, and one or more of my competitors are doing no work. Again, however, you are not there to please your fellow racers. Your goal is to stay safe and win the race.

If you enter a large road race as the USCF events often are here in Florida, it is extremely important to position yourself properly for the start. I coach a friend, Jerry Rush, an excellent climber. One of the most challenging races on the Florida schedule is the Sugar Loaf Race named after Sugar Loaf Mountain, an extremely steep, prolonged grade that must be negotiated four times during the rather long race. It is a climber's dream. I believed that Jerry could win the race in 2008 because of his training, his lack of road racing experience notwithstanding.

There was a very large field, and Jerry found himself towards the back of the pack at the start. Jerry slowly worked his way up through the pack during the almost two (2) hours of racing, and noted that each time Sugar Loaf Mountain was negotiated, he would easily pass numerous riders during the ascent. The finish line was very close to the final ascent, and Jerry was riding in about 20th place at the start of the last climb. He easily out-climbed his competitors, and reached the summit in what he thought was first place. Unfortunately, after finishing the race, he discovered that there had been a three-rider break-away early in the race that he was unaware of.

Prior to the start of large road races, organizers arrange the racers in a queue at the side of or on the road. This usually determines their starting position when called to the line. Get to that queue early to assure yourself a starting position near the front. In that way, you will be able to cover any breaks and perhaps be in position to stage one yourself.

Do not attempt a break away at the wrong time. The three state road race championships that I have won were by break-aways miles from the finish line. I was in a road race once in which I assumed that I would win because I was the best time trial rider in the race. Just prior to the road race there was a time trial event which I handily won. Because of that, when we rounded the last turn leading to the finish line, I thought that if I accelerated up to over 30 mph, none of the racers would be able to hold my wheel. As we approached the finish line, my main competition went flying by and later thanked me for allowing him to win the race with the free ride on my wheel. I was in the zone and unaware of him being right behind me. I had given him a perfect lead-out to beat me!

The lesson to be learned is that you should not attempt a break-away with the finish line in sight but too far from the finish to sustain an all-out sprint. If a person is able to grab your wheel, they will be doing about 30% less work than you, and will, undoubtedly, be able to sling shot off of your wheel. Ideally, be on another racer's wheel until you can commence an all-out sprint.

The most effective way to learn how to road race is to road race. Experience is the best teacher.

CHAPTER 22...

EPILOGUE: AFTER THE TIME TRIAL

I recently competed in the United States Cycling Federation's Florida State Time Trial championships. Although I won my division by one (1) minute and 50 seconds and set a new PR for 20K, I failed to practice what I preached.

In the chapter that dealt with time trial racing techniques, I discussed the pre-race meal indicating that it should be consumed at least three hours prior to the event. I further mentioned that my meal has evolved to being simply a Clif™ bar, banana, and a glass of water.

My starting time for the event was a rather late 11:56 a.m. and Rosie was right after me so we planned on breakfast at 8:00 a.m. I figured that with so many hours until the start I could modify my pre-race meal and the hotel had a great buffet available to the racers. I consumed a plate of and eggs, toast, OJ, fruit and a muffin. Oh, it felt and tasted so good!

About 15 minutes prior to our start—which was delayed by about 20 minutes--having warmed up for an hour and 40 minutes, the bacon was still on my stomach and I felt like I was going to throw up. Remember the phenomenon of the nervous pre-race stomach? Well, I did not upchuck, but I will never go off my planned pre- race eating routine in the future. My advice again is to not vary your pre-race meal routine simply because you have more time to digest it!

I would also like to give you an update on Dave Viney. This year,

2009, Dave upgraded his race bike. In his interval workouts he felt that he was going a bit faster than he had been going on his other bike. I also mentioned that Dave cycled an incredible time of 52:56 for 40 kilometers at the state meet last year. When he described his prodigious interval sessions to me and the incredible average power and speed that he was attaining, I told him that I expected him to race to a sub-52 minute performance this year.

The course this year was an ideal, accurately-measured, virtually-flat course. Dave turned in an absolutely incredible time of 50:46--a 29.4 mph average for almost 25 miles! It is amazing what this dedicated, 59 year old masters athlete and others can achieve with dedication, good training habits, and proper equipment. He is an inspiration to me and everyone who knows him!

Oh, by the way, I will be changing my eating habits the night before an important race: When I arrived at the event hotel in Jacksonville, FL, I discovered Dave in the lobby enjoying a plate of apple pie ala mode!

Finally, the event was a vindication of the training techniques that I have promulgated in past articles. I started training Rosie a few months ago using the program that I outline in this book. Although she has been competing for two years, she never underwent any formal, structured training. She accompanied me on my interval sessions and performed them very strictly taking virtually no rest interval between work intervals. The upshot was that she not only won the 2009 USCF, State of Florida, women's 60+ division, but cycled 20 kilometers at a faster rate of speed than she was capable of cycling a five (5) kilometer time trial just a few months before!

 # CHAPTER 23...

LEVELS IN SPORTS

I have always been intrigued by the phenomenon of levels in sports. My mission is not to write about the obvious levels in sports such as those demonstrated by the likes of Lance Armstrong and Michael Phelps, but to expound on the subject in relation to how levels tend to bring us personally back to our own sports reality, and, facing that reality, how we should respond.

My first "conscious awareness" of this subject was when I was an avid tennis player in the early 70s. I played almost daily at a tennis club in Forest Hills, NY. The club champion and runner-up were doubles partners and they would thrash any doubles team who had the audacity to challenge their prowess. They were the local club tennis "studs" and most of us coveted their skills. They entered a doubles tournament in New York City which I attended as a spectator. I was gleefully looking forward to watching others fall victim to their incredible skills. I was astounded as I watched them get soundly defeated by another team certainly well above their "A" player status. Levels!

My first "painful experiences" with levels in sports came about through my competitive running. I was a high school miler in the 50s, and I returned to the sport at the age of 34. My first goal was to break five (5) minutes for a mile. It was not a particularly easy task in that, to achieve that goal, I had to remove the barrier of the six-minute-mile. Finally, at a master's track meet on Randall's Island, NY, I clocked an incredibly painful, but delightfully exciting 4:57 time.

I was elated, and probably felt similar to Roger Banister the day he became the first person to break the four-minute-mile barrier. My elation was short lived when I read that Bill Rogers had just run 2:09:27 at the Boston Marathon equivalent to running twenty-six (26), 4:57 miles in a row without stopping! Levels!

My masters running career was becoming very successful, and I was winning many first-place age-group trophies and medals. I often finished among the top few places in large, open-road races. In 1979, I won my first sub-master prize (I was 39 at the time) in a cross country championship at the venerable course--known as "The Rock" for good cause--at Van Courtland Park in the Bronx, NY. It was a very difficult and comprised of two laps when the distance contested was 10 kilometers. Here I am, 30 years later, and I can still clearly see the race in unfolding and completing:

The start was on a grassy flat that led to a very difficult trek through narrow, climbing, twisting, blind turns strewn with vegetation and rocks. The footing was quite treacherous, and often, it was necessary to hurdle a fellow competitor who had fallen. The runner would pass through an area known as Cemetery Hill (it apparently was an old Indian burial ground) which I always thought was appropriately named based on the way I typically felt at that juncture of the race. Finally and mercifully, the runner entered the flats again only to be confronted by a repeat of the above described course negotiating lap two. It was most painful and, at the same time, exhilarating.

I finally turned 40, and I was enjoying many wins in the masters' category at various road and track running events. One of my career highlights was winning first-place masters' prize by a margin of 40 seconds at a road race with hundreds of participants covered by *Sports Illustrated*. One of my most enjoyable experiences was pacing prolific author, teammate, and cardiologist, Dr. George Sheehan (at that time, medical editor of *Runner's World* magazine) to an American, age-group record for 1,500 meters at the AAU Eastern Regional Masters' Track Championships at Princeton University. I was starting to think that I was a pretty darn good runner. I fantasized to myself, "I probably could have been an Olympian had I never stopped running after High School." I was however, about to get a first-hand, and very dramatic demonstration of the phenomenon of levels.

Fast forward to the cross country championships at Van Courtland Park the next year. I had trained very hard that year to win the gold as the masters' cross country champion. On race day, there were the usual familiar faces from the racing circuit except for one chap, a rather fit looking stranger. The gun sounded, and the aforementioned runner left the rest of the pack in the dust. I commented to another competitor with whom I had raced on numerous occasions, "This guy is going blow up very quickly."

I was soon running in second place (behind the breakaway runner), and when we entered the hills, I lost track of the runner in front of me due to all of the turns, trees, and brush. Finally, I broke out on to the flats, and my suspicion was confirmed – the other runner had apparently dropped out, and I was leading the race! I pushed myself wanting to post a good time, and entered the dreaded hills for the second 5K loop of the race.

The practice at this meet was for an official to hand an ice cream stick to each competitor as he finished, with his place embossed upon it. I made a last valiant sprint to better my winning time, contorted my face in an "enhanced" grimace for the benefit of the press and photographers, and fell to the ground clutching my first place stick. I lay there moaning and retching from the effort, and finally recovered enough to glance down at my stick which mistakenly sported the number "2" on it. I staggered over to one of the officials to point out the error, and gasped to him as I approached, "You gave me the wrong stick – I won the race and my stick says 2nd place." He pointed to my right at the runner who I thought had dropped out of the race and said, "<u>He</u> won the race."

Oscar Moore, a 1964 Olympian at five kilometers (5K) had not dropped out of the race, but had won by a substantial margin in a new masters' course record time. He had apparently never stopped running and was working as the track coach at Glassboro State University. He had trained hard for that championship event which was going to be his (very successful) masters running debut. I'm too embarrassed to tell you Mr. Moore's winning margin, but I had just gotten my best ever demonstration of Levels in Sports! I also got a close-up look at a true Olympian – not a wannabe such as myself! Levels!

So here you are, a hard-core competitor who is used to winning first place in your category at whatever sport you happen to participate in. The day of reckoning rears its ugly head and you come up against your equivalent of Oscar Moore in your next competition. What do you do? Do you give up because you must be the best? Do you get depressed or become impossible to live with? Do you find another sport? The answer is "none of the above." We must each realize and acknowledge that there is always someone who is going to be faster, better, more skilled, etc. We must turn the experience into something positive. Let the phenomenon of levels work for you – not discourage you.

After my ill-fated meeting with Oscar Moore, I trained even harder than before, and I continued to set personal bests in subsequent years. Unfortunately, I never met the chap again in competition. Had that happened, he might have defeated me, but I can guarantee you that it would have been by a much lesser margin than our first meeting. I might have even kicked his butt!

In March of 2005, I had been cycling for just a few months, and, much to my glee, I discovered that I apparently had good genetics for the sport. I was "hanging" with the fast boys and started to consider the possibility of competing. I decided to enter one of the many Senior Games events offered throughout the year in Florida, and decided on an out-of-the-way venue where I could probably start my racing career with a win. The event was a five kilometer (5K) time trial. I raced my heart out that day only to discover that not only did I not win (I took second), but I had lost by 33 seconds over a rather short distance! "Maybe bicycle racing was not for me," I thought as a silver medal— the first loser in my mind-- was hung around my neck.

The man who had defeated me was Leon Burk, a multiple-state and national time trial and road race champion who had broken numerous time trial records. In that obscure venue, I had stumbled on to a competition with one of the best racers in the country in my age group! As an aside, Leon is one of the most incredible gentlemen one could ever hope to meet. He is the prototype of a friendly, quiet, low-key and unassumingly-modest kind of guy—and so fast on a bike! He is the type of bike racing friend you meet who you almost don't want to defeat.

I had run into another example of levels at that race, and learned the lesson that every race can be so different and unpredictable, but I used it to inspire me rather than discourage me. After all, I had less than one year of racing and he had more than 20 of multi-sport competitions. I vowed that I would train diligently and set my goals high and someday – although it seemed an impossible dream at the time – defeat Leon in a time trial race. I kept a picture of him riding his time trial bike on my computer. Finally a year and 10 months subsequent to the first meeting, I defeated Leon in a 5K time trial. The margin was a mere three seconds, but I was elated.

Off the subject of levels for a moment--Let your defeats and failures inspire you. I mentioned in an earlier article dealing with the subject of time trial racing, that at the 2007 Senior Olympics, I went off course in a 10K time trial that I was sure I would win. I must honestly say that I still cannot help but thinking, "what if," but I used the incident to inspire me to become a better cyclist. I trained harder than ever, and as of this writing, I have not lost another time trial in a year and nine (9) months since the incident at the Olympics.

Train hard, treat your losses as inspirational fodder, and, perhaps, someday a competitor will tell the tale of the time he or she crossed your path only to have the phenomenon of levels painfully demonstrated to him or her!

CHAPTER 24...

TURN YOUR DEFEATS INTO SUCCESS

In 2007, I had numerous goals. I wanted to win the USCF Florida state time trial and road race championships; win a gold medal at the Senior Olympics; and win both time trials at the Florida State Senior Games Championships. I also wanted to break both state time trial records. The goal that meant the most to me, however, was a win at the Senior Olympics. The NSGA, National Senior Games Association, oversees the senior games for the various states. The Senior Olympics is the national championships for the Senior Games system. One must qualify to compete at the Senior Olympics by placing first or second at one of the state championships held annually by each state.

I was training very hard leading up to the Olympics and I was fortunate in that the two USCF Florida state championships--time trials and road races--were being held earlier in the same month as the Olympics. It was the perfect schedule to reach a razor-sharp peak by the time I toed the line for the first time trial event at the Olympics.

I was very confident going into the Olympics. My training was right on schedule, and I was winning events with fast times. I also had defeated a couple of national champions. My confidence however, waned rather drastically when I saw that the time trials at the Olympics were going to be held on technical, hilly courses in Cherokee Park in Louisville. I had won the state road race on a single breakaway, and, just six (6) days prior to the Olympics, I won the USCF Florida state time trial championship by a rather wide margin and turned in the fastest time for 20 kilometers by over two (2) minutes than had previously been ridden at the state meet for my age group, 65-69. I was ready!

The day before the first event, the 5K time trial, I became very discouraged as I did some practice runs on the course with three very good time trial riders from Florida. The course started on the flats, but then commenced a downhill section where it was quite easy to attain speeds of around 31-32 mph. As the terrain leveled off, it was necessary to negotiate a rather narrow, blind left turn on to a two-lane roadway. One lane would be in use by racers who had reached the turnaround point and were heading back towards the finish. At the point that the turn needed to be negotiated, the actual lane that the racer needed to turn onto was virtually obscured by virtue of the camber of the road. If the racer turned wide, he would go down a steep, grassy embankment; if he turned short, he would come in conflict with racers going the opposite direction.

My forte is not bike handling. I am envious of my son, Chris, a track racer, and Rosie's son, Ian, an ex-professional, triathlete, who can do all kinds of acrobatic-type moves on their bikes. I do okay on a road bike, but on a time trial bike with its aero configuration and disk wheel, I don't seem to be able to hold a straight line very well. I jokingly tell people that I ride about 21 kilometers when I race a 20K race! I am only half joking, however, and I think it is a result of the accident that broke my neck. I became more cautious when racing around a turn.

My three training partners were able to negotiate the turn at full speed, and I found it necessary to slow to a maximum speed of around 17 mph to successfully and safely negotiate the turn. Unfortunately, after the turn, there was a prolonged climb to the turnaround point. Those who were able to maintain their speed from the previous downgrade had adequate momentum to make the ensuing climb rather easy. Those who bogged down, such as me, were in for some pain. I practiced a few times, but I could never efficiently make that turn.

On race day, my adrenalin carried me to a very fast downhill segment, but when I reached that dreaded turn, it looked even worse than it had during practice. Now there were red cones seemingly everywhere in the roadway, and racers were coming from the other direction. I braked hard for the turn, and then suffered greatly as I started climbing. The bottom line was that I turned what I considered a depressing 4th place out of 59 racers.

The man who won was someone I had defeated numerous times including about a month before the Olympics and then again four (4) months afterward. Understand that I am not whining and issuing disclaimers. The course was a true measure of a champion and the winner soundly defeated me by eight (8) seconds. It was however, one of the most disappointing moments of my life.

As they played the Olympic Fanfare at the awards ceremony and I was handed my fourth place ribbon, depression is the most accurate description of my mood. I have a picture of lineup of the first seven (7) finishers and the guy who finished one place behind me has his down-turned thumb over my head. I remember him congratulating me, and I can't recall what I said to him, but it was something to the effect that I had done nothing worthy of being congratulated for.

The 10K time trial was to be contested in three (3) more days, but, before that, the 40K road race was scheduled. I decided to scratch from that race to put a full effort towards winning the 10K time trial which was on a course more suited to my riding skills. On the morning of the 10K race, I felt like I could tear the cranks off of the bike. Unfortunately, it was not to be.

This is how I described the race in an email I sent to a friend that night:

"Here is what happened at today's 10K time trial championships. I knew I was coming to the line in peak form, and in spite of the very technical, hilly course, I wanted that national championship badly. I took a good hour and a half warm-up and with a start time of 11:28, I arrived at the line just four (4) minutes prior to liftoff with a nicely warmed up engine ready to do battle. I came off the line, and after accelerating up to about 27 mph, I settled on to the aero bars and started working. I hit 34.3 mph on the first down grade, and literally flew up the first hill. I sensed I was in the zone, and the smile that formed on my face did not agree with my heart rate monitor which was indicating over a 170 clicks per minute. I, however, was feeling no pain, and I just knew that no one in the 59 man field in my five-year age group could take me today. I almost bought it on one turn when I came in too hot, and in my tunnel vision state not realizing how sharp of a turn it was. I almost took out a concrete bridge, but that simply plied my body with a well needed shot of adrenalin.

My 30 second man was a great racer from Texas. I was well aware of his capabilities, because I had checked out the Texas state results with the intention of going there to win their state championships during a visit to my and Rosie's sons and her daughter. I caught him just prior to the turn around point. I noted that I had closed on the defending national champion, and I knew that it was going to be a great day. I started back to the finish line with no lactic acid, and even though my heart rate was apparently touching the red line, I felt no pain - I was in the zone!

Every street that intersected the course had barricades across the roadway to preclude racers taking the incorrect route. I came flying around one turn at about 30 mph, and was suddenly confronted with a street full of red cones, two officials standing there gazing at me, and a roadway to my right with no barricade. I went flying down that steep roadway only to discover the ultimate nightmare - at the bottom of this steep road where barricades blocking the street. I had gone off course.

I had not only gone off course, but had to do it on a steep roadway necessitating some serious braking, and the subsequent climb back up the street (again, very steep), put me in not only severe oxygen debt, but severe mental debt. I quickly overcame the latter, because I knew that even though I had just wasted probably 30 seconds going up and down the street, and the time that I lost by not going down the proper route (a double penalty when you do something as stupid as I did), I was still running a very fast time. Unfortunately, a place where I had been doing 30 mph seconds before, I was now doing virtually zero with oxygen debt due to my climb back to the course route.

I dug very deeply into my being, and never let my speed fall off. I came over the finish line quite fast and commenced my retching ritual which lasted much longer than usual. Oh, and yes, for the first time ever, I did some retching while still out on the course. I had taken my body well beyond its limits.

The current Florida record for my age group is 16 flat. With running off the course, I ran an amazing 14:41 which is about a 25.4 mph average on a technical hilly course. The gold medalist from VA ran a great time of 14.20, so I lost the national championship by 21 seconds, and I sincerely believe I not only wasted much more than that with my excursion, but used up vital energy getting back on course.

As an aside, my poor 30 second man seeing me coming back up the street also went off course in spite of me using the last once of oxygen available to me to yell and point to him. The officials simply watched all of this transpire.

I was depressed to say the least. Rosie was trying to convince me that we do this for fun. I am trying to convince her that competition is life and death. Perhaps the truth lies somewhere between my hard-core approach and her Pollyanna approach."

This is Rosie and I can tell you that it was a disturbing sight to see a grown man with his head in his hands, sitting on the ground, totally dejected, feeling sorry for himself after a great race. Sometimes we have to lose to win. That was the end of any fun we might have had at the games.

I had a lot of press back in 2006 having come back from the broken neck. The first day we were at the Olympics, The Villages community had a full page ad in its newspaper with a full- page picture of my time trialing there the previous month. I had also given an interview which separately made the paper with another picture of me racing. I wished I were as good a cyclist as my press agent was a press agent!

If I thought I felt badly after losing the 5K title, I was totally and irrevocably down in the dumps now. To this day, I think about that race. I had one more chance to redeem myself at the Olympics – the 20K road race.

I practiced on the course the day before, and being a Florida boy used to riding and racing on the flats, I was getting a bit nervous about racing that hilly, technical course in Louisville. I was having difficulty with some turns after a down hill run, and I was all by myself. The thought of making them in traffic had me a bit concerned – especially considering the fact that I had finished my healing from a broken neck only about a year before.

There were close to 60 racers in our five-year age group, and the officials got us off to a safe start by pacing us through the first downhill and turn with a motorcycle. They then let us loose. As we flew down the next hill with racers on all sides of me negotiating a turn at over 30 mph, I thought, "This is not going to work for me." I felt so strong and I felt so much in danger on that course racing with people that I did not know, that I decided to go to the front of the peloton.

Now any sensible road racer knows if you go to the front of the peloton for anything other than a brief stay, you are not running a smart race. I now know that you either take your brief turn at the front, or you go for a total breakaway if you think you can pull it off. I stupidly pulled most of the race safely at the front, only to be passed by numerous riders as we did the last climb towards the finish line. I had expended too much energy to respond.

I was an abject failure—zero for three! The Senior Olympics is the best thing that ever happened to me vis-à-vis racing a bicycle! When I was finished licking my wounds (they were deep and numerous and it was a time consuming process), I made the decision that I would never again lose a bicycle race. I threw myself into my training with a vengeance. In calendar year 2008, I did not miss a single day of training and as I write this, I have missed one day in the last year and a half.

Five (5) months later, I not only went on to win both the 5K & 10K Florida State Senior Games championships, but set state records in both events. I broke the 10K record by 30 seconds. Two years out from that Olympic debacle, I have not lost a race and I have won six (6) Florida state cycling championships since then. I intend to win a lot more.

The lesson that I am trying to convey, admittedly in a rather verbose fashion, is that you must turn your defeats into success. Use your defeats to motivate you to higher levels of athletic performance. I have seen a couple of really good athletes walk away from the sport when they found themselves suddenly getting defeated. Walk towards it – not away from it!

CHAPTER 25...

NEVER GIVE UP

An incident that recently took place at the end of our club ride drove home to me the meaning of the adage, "Never Give Up." I'm as competitive as one can be, but even someone as hard-core as I can sometimes forget. Let me start however with a story from two years ago.

The 2007 USCF Florida state road race championships for my age group had a start time of 3:00 PM on a very humid day with temperatures in the high 90s and no wind. Apparently not thinking very clearly, I drove to the race venue with only one bottle of water assuming that there would be water available at the race site which, it turned out, was on a country road in the midst of a horse farm. Much to my dismay, all of the water supplied by the race organizer was gone, and there was no place to get any.

As I warmed up, I rationed my remaining water. As a result, by the time I got to the starting line, my heart rate was an elevated 137 (my resting pulse is 42), and I had very little water left. I knew that I was in for a long, painful day.

Our group was scheduled to ride with the masters women 40+ age group, and very quickly a four-person breakaway formed with two of the women, me and my main competitor. I came into the race at a very fit, 5' 11", 149 pounds with very little body fat. My main competitor was a wisp of a guy who weighed under 130 and kept attacking me on every hill. I was out of water, felt dehydrated, and at the end of the first lap, I had no idea how I would be able to last for another four. Spectators later informed me that I looked terrible.

Negative thoughts clouded my brain which was quite occupied creating stress for the lack of water and my increasing state of dehydration. I was sure that I would not be able to win the race. It never occurred to me that my competition might be feeling worse. The four of us stayed together swapping pulls and, about half way through the last lap, I was wondering if I could make it to the end without getting dropped. I had all but conceded the state championship. You would have to know me to understand how totally out of character that is for me.

Suddenly, both one of the women and my competitor threw up, one very quickly followed by the other. With only four (4) miles left to the finish, I seized the opportunity, tore off the front, and won the race by a large margin!

My fellow competitor later admitted to me that each time he would attack me on the hills, he was punishing himself more than he was me. As an aside, the conditions that day were so brutal that, at the end of the race, I needed an IV. I could not urinate for about 24 hours, and the next morning, I was still 5 pounds lighter than I was the morning of the race. Of course there are two lessons to be learned – hydrate adequately, and never give up!

As I mentioned earlier, my reason for writing this is an experience I had on our local club ride. It was a great demonstration of the "Never Give Up" adage. Our club rides are divided into various groups defined by the speeds that one must be able to sustain. There are a couple of very slow groups and there are 18-, 20-, 22-, 24- and 26-mph groups. I rode with the latter which often has sustained, non-sprint speeds of 32-33 mph.

At the time of the ride, I was in a peaking process in preparation for our state time trial championships, and I was coming into form very nicely. My plan was to do a lot of the work on the ride. I did numerous pulls, and with two miles to go and feeling very strong, I went off the front in an attempt to hold off the peloton to the end of the final sprint zone. I was holding about 28 mph, and in a couple of minutes I was joined by a group of three riders who had bridged up to me. I swapped pulls with one of them, and one of the group finally fell off the back.

We had about three-quarters of a mile to go to the end of the final sprint zone. As an aside, at the age of 69, I was the oldest rider in the group by probably 15 years. I had done more than my share of the work during the ride, and I was on the wheel of a bicycle racer in his early 20s. Suddenly a guy went flying by us. I commented to the chap pulling, "where did he come from? I guess he is going to win the sprint." His reply was, 'let's not give up – we can catch him.'"

Although it seemed an impossibility based upon the speed differential and the energy that we had already expended, off we went with me sucking his wheel. I thought that I had nothing left but suddenly with the excitement of the chase, I felt newly energized and said to the guy whose wheel I was following, "I'll lead you out and you can contest the sprint." I went to the front and closed on the guy who had passed us. He suddenly sat up, and I rode the other guy--who I was going lead out--off my wheel and won the sprint by a wide margin!

Never give up! I thought I had an empty tank, and it was not. If you are not hurting, you probably are not racing hard enough. Assume that your competitors are experiencing at least much pain as you, but I think a better strategy is to assume they are experiencing more! Don't assume that you have nothing left even if you feel that to be the case. Never, ever give up! I can assure you that if you are racing against me, I won't!

CHAPTER 26...

FAVORITE CYCLING TIPS

*It's a Matter of Thinking, Sometimes…*Rosie spent at least 30 minutes recently trying to pump up her bicycle tires on her road bike so that she could test out her new saddle position. After approximately 30 minutes of trying to get the air to stop coming out of the pump instead of going into the tire, she got on her time trial bike and headed out for her ride.

She met me on the Pinellas Trail on my way home and spewed forth this information while I was going over the bridge, heading for home after a 70 mile bike ride. Needless to say, I was not really listening and, when she turned around and followed me home, Jerry, my training partner, came with her and proceeded to try to pump up the tire. It did not work. She thought it was the stem leaking. I suggested, with a superior attitude that perhaps she should try to pump up another tire. Sometimes I am so smart….

The problem, it turned out, was in the pump head and not something that she or anyone else unfamiliar with bike maintenance would likely think of. It should be noted that she had recently mastered the technique of putting air in her tires with this fairly new, easy-to-use pump. If you are a small person, it is very difficult to get a regular tire pump up to 120 psi without jumping up and down on it.

So, sometimes solutions to every day problems we encounter on our bikes require patience, wisdom, perseverance and, many times, advice from friends. It is, indeed, a matter of thinking—of all the possibilities on this relatively-simple mechanical device.

To be sure, there are probably many of you who will say, "I have an even better way to do that!" Please share it if you do. Following our helpful hints you will find contributions from friends and family who were asked to contribute to this ever-changing list.

Group Riding:

If you watch road racing, you will note that the professional racers appear to be so close to one another that you wonder how they can avoid crashing. They drink, eat, and talk while riding at high speeds. For all of the miles they ride, there are surprisingly few crashes because they are all professionals and working together for safety's sake. Also, they have years of riding at greater than 25 miles per hour for many miles.

In club rides, if you are a regular participant, you will have an opportunity to get to know your fellow riders. You know who is strong and will do a long pull and those that will sit back and relax and go along for the ride.

Your safety week after week is pretty much determined by whether or not a new rider comes into the group that might not know how you usually ride together. It only takes one wrong move to put a number of people in jeopardy. Some basic rules to follow as courtesy would dictate when riding for pleasure with friends or racing in a group of strangers are:

- Try to be the rider that others enjoy being with.

- Hold your line.

- Don't stop pedaling every few seconds—soft pedal rather than stop pedaling.

- Don't chatter endlessly about nothing.

- Leave your radio at home or don't use it on the group ride.

- Don't use your brakes in other than an emergency situation. For traffic stops, call out: "stopping" or "slowing" so the riders behind you can respond versus react. A hand placed on the back, also conveys the fact that your are slowing.

- Learn the technique of gently "feathering" your brakes if necessary.

- When it is your turn to pull through in a pace line, do just that —if you are incapable of doing so, get out of the pace line—you don't belong in it. If you feel weak on a particular day, just make your pull brief.

- Don't suddenly drop off a wheel in front of you leaving the guy behind to close a large gap. Drop off in time to warn the rider in back that you are about to do so.

- Don't play peloton policeman.

- Do Not Overlap Wheels! Do ride slightly off centered from the wheel in front of you so that there is a margin of error should the rider in front of you suddenly slow down. It is the person in the rear that usually gets hurt the most.

- In tight spots, announce when you are passing another rider in the group, i.e., "Passing on your left."

- Have situational awareness – know what's going on around you.

- Don't show up every day with the same irritating noises emanating from your bike – fix it or have it fixed.

- Wear a helmet – you might think you are cool to ride helmetless, but you come off like a jerk—and clip the strap!

- Do your share of the work—don't always be a "wheel sucker" in a group that is too fast for you every week. Join a slower group and work yourself up to the next level.

- Don't let another rider pull you for extended periods and then go sprinting by that rider as your approach the end of the sprint zone. It is not polite.

- If you lose a sprint, save your disclaimers for someone interested which will not be the person who defeated you or the other riders in the group.

- Do not ride in a group with a bike in a state of disrepair. It is an accident waiting to happen.

- When the group has settled into a certain pace, do not increase the pace when it is your turn to pull unless you specifically plan to attack.

- When you want to give up your pull, pat your hip or flip your elbow and pull off to the left while slightly slowing to let the group pass you. Return to the group either where there is a break or at the end of the pace line.

- When the next person is ready to give up the pull, let him or her know you are the "last" person so that he or she knows when to cut back in.

- Do not use your aero-bars while riding in a group if you use the same bike for time trials or triathlons. It amazes me when people try to justify so doing by claiming the ability to immediately transition from riding on aero bars to their brake levers located a distance from their hands. No one is interested in your alleged expertise; it is dangerous to use them in a group. That is why they are not allowed when you are racing in USCF or Senior Games.

- Introduce yourself to new riders who come into your group – make them feel comfortable and welcome.

- Point out obstacles on the road to the riders behind you by pointing down with your right hand. Shout out things like: "bump," "sand," "water," "glass," and potentially conflicting traffic to the other riders.

- Stop for people who experience flats and other mechanical problems – at least make sure that someone will be there to assist if help is needed.

- When leading the pack and making a sharp turn, slow down a bit to allow the group to catch up. Remember that the riders in the back get slowed down by the "accordion effect." Do the same at toll booths and other areas that tend to funnel the riders into a smaller space.

- Be aware of where your ride is going. If you are going on a long ride where you are unfamiliar with the route, let someone in the group know so that they will not abandon you if you get dropped.

- Don't needlessly antagonize automobile drivers - a car can hurt or kill you, and so can a stressed driver equipped with a weapon.

Punctures, Tire, and Wheel Problems:

- Carry a tool kit and have latex gloves, an air cartridge, a small rag, some Allen wrenches, and a tool to take your tire off of the rim. Don't plan on someone being around who is prepared to help you. If you do not have a tire removal tool, use the clip end of your skewer to slip under the tire. A skewer lever can be a good makeshift tire lever.

  Before you put the new tube into the tire, run a rag around the inside of the tire to check for any glass. Also do a careful visual inspection. Then, put a small amount of air in your tube and insert it into the tire being careful that it does not get twisted. Put one side of the tire and tube onto the rim being careful not to twist the tube; insert the front part of the tire into the rim taking care not to leave any tube between the tire and the rim (which might later create a pinch blowout!). Starting at the valve stem, slowly rotate the tire 360 degrees pushing the tire inwards and make sure that you cannot see any tube showing hence assuring yourself that no part of the tube will be trapped under the bead of the tire. Do that on both sides of the tire. Then blow up your tire.

- When searching for an elusive puncture to a tube, submerge the tube in water and slowly rotate it until you see bubbles coming from the spot(s) that is leaking.

  Rather than filling up a sink up with water, simply remove the top from the tank on your toilet, and rotate the tube in the tank. It's faster and saves water.

- Prior to removing the rear wheel of your bicycle, shift to the small chain ring and the smallest cog prior to removing the wheel. This will make it much easier to replace the wheel by simply positioning the chain to align with the smallest cog prior to pushing the wheel into place.

- Inspect your tires after every ride, looking for small items such as chards of glass embedded in the rubber. Gently remove them with a small, pointed tool such as an awl or a tweezers. You will save yourself lots of flat tires over time.

- Wheels that make squeaking noises often do so due to the skewers being too loose. If you are running deep-dish, carbon wheels, a common source of noise is a valve stem extender clicking against the rim. Simply place a piece of electrical tape over the extension, and secure it to the wheel.

- The ballpark numbers for the wheel circumference often suggested by bicycle computer manufacturers are often not very close to the real number.

  (1) Measure your wheel by inflating your tires to the amount you typically use.

  (2) Mark a spot on the ground, for example, by the valve stem which should be sitting in the six o'clock position.

  (3) With your weight on the bicycle, slowly roll your bike for three (3) wheel revolutions until, on the third rotation, the valve stem stops at the 6 o'clock position.

  (4) Mark that spot, measure the distance between the two marks in millimeters, divide by three (3), and the resultant number is the one that you should put in your computer.

If you use two different wheel sets on the bike, measure each separately and install one number as the "A" reading and the other as the "B" reading. Most computers will accommodate readings for two bicycles (or sets of wheels).

- Shoe Goo is an excellent product designed to be put on the heel area of running shoes to make them last longer. I use it to fill in little cuts and holes in my tires when I check them after every ride.

Tubular Tires:

When I first started riding bicycles, the owner of the store advised me that the best place to efficiently save weight on a bicycle is to use lighter components that rotate. Rotational weight savings pay the biggest performance dividend. Examples of components where rotational weight can be saved are:

- Wheels
- Tires
- Pedals (titanium)
- Cranks
- Drive-train Components

I always wanted to use tubular tires, but I was not willing to face the hassle of the seemingly-complicated, messy process of gluing a tire on to a wheel rim. I wanted not only the weight savings afforded by these wheels (a set of Zipp 404 tubular wheels weigh 1232 grams versus a set of clincher 404 wheels which weigh 1615 grams), but also the enhanced ride and handling. I also wanted to be able to use higher tire pressure for time trial racing—another advantage of tubular tires. I then discovered that there is an alternative to gluing—tape.

Tufo produces a line of two-sided tire tape that is very quickly an easily applied to the rim of the wheel. It is just, if not more, efficient than glue. I actually find it more difficult removing a tire from a rim that has been taped versus one that has been glued.

Some argue that tubular tires are more of a hassle when one suffers a flat tire. I actually find it easier. Vittoria Pit Stop is a wonderful product that very quickly and efficiently not only repairs minor flat-causing cuts to the tire, but also inflates the tire to 120 psi. Tufo also manufacturers an excellent elongated tool bag that easily carries a can of Pit Stop and even a spare tire and tape for those who like to ride fully equipped as I do. It fits nicely behind the seat.

Don't deny yourself the wonders of tubular tires because of perceived difficulty of use.

Chain, Derailleur, Chain Rings, Cogs:

Chain Wear and Sizing:

Your chain should be regularly checked for wear. Cyclists often erroneously believe that a bicycle chain stretches, and, when it stretches beyond a certain limit, it must be replaced.

The chain itself does not stretch—the rollers wear out and causes the distance between links to become longer. A worn chain will cause poor shifting and needless wear on the drive train. A new chain measures exactly one (1) inch per link. An easy measure of a chain's wear is to use a 12" ruler. The one inch mark is placed at the center of one rivet, and the 12" mark should align exactly with the center of the 24th rivet, or end rivet on the 12th link. A chain which is within 1/16th of an inch of that 12-inch measurement is okay. If the chain measures between 1/16th and 1/8th of an inch longer than the specified 12-inch distance, replace the chain.

Park Tool Company manufactures two chain-wear measurement devices for quick and accurate measurement of chain wear. One is sort of a "go-or-no-go" device, and the other is a bit more precise in measuring the exact amount of wear. I have them both, and they are excellent, handy tools.

When you take a new chain out of the box, understand that the stock size is probably not the size needed for your particular bicycle. There are basically three accurate ways to determine the length of the chain that your bicycle needs:

1. The easiest method: Compare the new chain to the old chain length (assuming it was accurately installed in the first place), and use the exact number of links for the replacement. Note that length, or number of links in your maintenance records to alleviate the need for future measurements.

2. Use a chain length calculator. Here is a link to an excellent on-line chain length calculator: http://www.Machinehead-software.co.uk/bike/chain_length/chainlengthcalc.html

3. Remove the old chain.

   - Shift the front derailleur over the smallest largest chain ring and the rear derailleur on the smallest cog.

   - Thread the new chain through the front derailleur. It is not necessary to thread the chain through the rear derailleur at this point. Simply wrap the chain around the largest front chain ring and around the largest rear cog.

   - Pull the chain tight, and note the closest rivet where the two could be joined. Keep in mind a chain can only be joined by mating inner and outer plates.

   - From the closet rivet, lengthen the chain by counting over an additional two rivets (two links), which is a distance of one-inch. "Break" the chain at this point.

- Remove the chain from the bike and thread it through the derailleur and join the ends.

Remember, clean and lube your chain on a regular basis and it will reward you with smooth, maximum power.

- When you oil your chain, place the drops of oil on the side of the chain that contacts the chain rings/cogs. In other words: oil the top side of the bottom part of the chain. Run your chain for a few revolutions to work the lube into the rollers, and, after allowing the chain lube to "cure" for a few hours, thoroughly wipe down the sides and top/bottom of the chain to remove excessive oil.

- If your rear derailleur is not shifting properly, adjust the barrel adjustment on the rear of the derailleur in the direction that the chain is improperly shifting. For example, if it is difficult to shift to a lower gear (larger cog), turn the barrel adjustment counter clockwise (tightening the cable).

General Bicycle Tips:

- If you get saddle sores, use Preparation H™ on the sores. It really helps!

- When your bike is properly fitted, keep a record of various important measurements such as the distance from the center of the bottom bracket to the top of the seat with the tape running along the seat tube; the distance of the rear of your seat to the front of your stem, etc.

- Record all of your rides using a good computer program. I recommend CycliStats™ as the absolutely best program available. You can download a trial copy at http://www. shastasoftware.com/CycliStats/index.htm

- Two of my favorite websites for maintenance information are parktool.com and sheldonbrown.com.

- Do not wear a championship jersey that you have not earned.

- When storing your bicycle for prolonged periods, leave your chain on the smallest front and rear ring/cog. It relieves pressure on the derailleur springs and prevents them from stretching.

- If you want to be taken seriously as a Roadie, shave your legs. Riders will proclaim that they do it to make it easier to receive massages and rub on sunscreen. Some proclaim that it is easier to treat road rash with shaved legs. The real reason, however, for non-pros shaving their legs is peer pressure – a very strong force!

- After riding through some debris or glass on the road that has a good chance of causing a flat, if you can do it easily, reach down to the front tire in front of the brakes and lightly touch your glove to the rolling wheel. If there is any glass or debris sticking out of the tire waiting to work its way in to cause a puncture, you will dislodge it.
  If you cannot comfortably do this, stop and get off of your bike and do both wheels.

Cleaning Chains and Cogs:

- Use any good degreaser such as Greased Lightning™ or Simple Green™ to clean your chain. Put your bike on a rack, rotate the chain forward, and spray while you hold a rag or paper towel under the chain. It is simple and not as messy as using a chain cleaner.

- Use large pipe cleaners to get in between the links and also to clean around the barrel, rear wheel cassette, and cogs.

- Use a toothbrush soaked in degreaser to get excess grease off of the chain.

Tips from Chris Scott, Sandy's son, a champion track cyclist in Texas:

- On-the-Bike Quad & Hip Flexor Stretch: While rolling, un-clip one foot, and place the top of your foot on your seat (as if you were going to sit on your shoe) and point your knee towards the road. You'll get a good stretch without having to get off the bike. Repeat for the other leg.

- When inflating your tires before a ride, don't pump higher than the desired pressure with the intent of making up for the air that is lost when you disconnect from the valve. The air you hear escaping is from the pressure in the pump hose, not your tires.

- When riding in a group, holding your line is important. Nobody wants to ride with someone who is erratic or unpredictable, no matter how fast you are

- You probably didn't "beat" the fast guy on your group ride. Chances are the he just raced the day before and this is his fun recovery spin :).
- If you are at least a semi-serious rider and can afford a power meter, get one. You'll quickly realize how worthless your previous bike computer equipment was.

Tips from: Ian Ray, Rosie's son. Past member: U.S.A. National Resident Team, Triathlon, Olympic Training Center, 2001, 2002. Champion triathlete and retired pro.

On Training:

- Listen to your body. Don't overdo it. Only increment your mileage

10-15% per training period; i.e., on a daily; weekly; monthly; or yearly basis.

- Drink the same fluids you will have in a race while you train so that your body becomes accustomed to them.

- Stay with your training limits when you go out with a group or with a cycling buddy. Do not get into a race when you are supposed to be doing active rest.

- If you have separate bikes for road racing and time trials, ride your time trial bike often and not just a few days before a race. My body needs the "muscle memory" to improve my TT racing. Perhaps yours does also.

- Hydrate before an event and stay hydrated up to the race day. Your body does not get hydrated two hours before your race.

Racing:

- Don't try anything new on race day—food, clothing, drinks, bike, etc.

- Visualize something powerful that goes fast, like a train or a horse, while you are hurting. It will help you to focus and ignore the pain.
- If you are doing a long race, have a good breakfast three (3) hours before. I like protein and carbohydrates such as eggs and toast.

- Go as hard as you can until you feel as if you are going to cramp, then, fall back a bit. Focus on your form, strategy, effort, and technique which are the factors you can control while racing. Don't worry about your competitors.

Transporting Bikes:

- Use foam insulation sheets from Home Depot which you can cut and use to cover the tubes. Wrap the derailleur in bubble wrap and tape it securely.

Tips from Gary Carr – Multiple-States' Time Trial and Road Race Champion - Senior Games

Chronic Back Pain Relief:

- Since I have chronic back pain, I have developed a way of relieving the pain when it develops during the ride without getting off the bike and stretching. While riding in an upright position with my hands on the handlebars, I arch my back for 10 seconds and then try to round the back for 10 seconds. I repeat that routine for 10 reps. I have found that I can do this at about any time during the ride--even while in a pace line--and the important thing is that the pain is gone when I am done with the routine.

Getting Aero Without Aerobars:

- I use my handle bars and brake hoods as a replacement which allows me to get into a more aerodynamic position rather than getting all the way down on the handlebar drops. My back is flat and my elbows are in and I develop much more power while in the tucked position. By moving back a little further on the saddle, this position is very effective for hill climbing.

Riding on Hot Oil and Chip Country Roads:

- For riders that ride on oil and chip country roads: In hot weather when the road oil bubbles up and sticks to the bike tires, I have found that using an old credit card or similar piece of plastic works well to scrape off the oil and rocks that may have stuck to the tires without damaging the tires.

- **General Tips from Friends:** I also steer away from typical cleaning solutions for the bike. Instead of overpriced-foaming-miracle-cleaners I use furniture polish. You can buy it for 99 cents at your local Big Lots. It makes your bike shiny and smells lemony fresh.

- Re-wrap your handlebars often. Most folks don't realize how corrosive sweat is. By changing tape often you'll be able to better monitor the condition of your bars. We have a club member who rides every day and his handlebars broke. That wouldn't have happened had he not ridden the same sweat-saturated bar-tape for so long. Tape is cheap enough (usually $10-$15) and only takes a few minutes to replace.

- How do you justify spending upwards of $3000 on a bike to someone who doesn't ride? You can't. The solution for me: Turn them into a cyclist. "It only took a few rides and my mom was hooked. That made equipment upgrades a whole lot easier! Now the whole family rides. It's such a joy to go for a spin flanked by my mother, sister and step-father. This is something I'm sure you can understand!"

- When laying your bicycle down, always lay it on the left side to prevent getting dirt in the drive train and/or bending the rear derailleur. For putting cream on your butt--skip the exotic and pricey rubs you see in bike shops.

- Install your bicycle computer sensor on the right side of the bicycle. That way, when you follow my recommendation to lay your bike on the left side, your sensor is protected from being moved from its proper distance from the wheel.

- If your chain comes off one of the front sprockets, typically there will be no need to get off the bike to put the chain back on to the chain ring. Simply shift the front derailleur as if you were attempting to shift on to the large chain ring, and the chain will typically correctly position itself. There is no need to get your hands greasy.

- Try **JR Watkins Apothecary Burn Cream™.** A customer handed me a jar last year and said, "try this- you'll never use anything else". He was right. JR Watkins Burn Cream contains Lidocaine. Not only does it stop chaffing through reduced friction but it numbs your underside as you ride. I'll never climb aboard a bike without it! JR's burn Cream is only $5.99 per jar compared to other brands which get upward of $25 for the same amount of product.

CHAPTER 27...

FAVORITE CYCLING PRODUCTS

As a couple, we have bought a lot of bikes over the past few years and have, consequently, built up an excellent list of vendors we rely on for our simple maintenance. I have taught Rosie how to pump up a tire, change a flat, grease her chains, and clean and grease the pedals. Some of the other things that I do in my personal bicycle maintenance area are: changing cassettes, chains, bottom brackets, brake pads and making various adjustments to the bike. I do leave the "serious" stuff for the experts.

For simplicity and economy, we try to use the same products and I generally pick them out. The only piece of hardware that we had unexpected problems with was one of the many bike pumps we have purchased, tried more than a few times, and then put it aside (see below).

If you have not guessed it yet, I am driven by knowledge and will get on the Internet or read books and magazines that will give me the best-of-the-best products for our use. Having suffered a broken neck, I do not need a fork that breaks or a wheel that shatters. Research is fun and has worked to our benefit.

These vendors highlighted here have proven over the years that they care about customer service and take pride in communicating with their customers directly. For the most part, they will answer your call or email for information promptly. We do not have to talk to someone overseas nor do we have to beg them to take care of problems and their products are great. We hope that you can benefit from our experiences with these fine companies.

SpeedPlay Zero Pedals™ – When I had been cycling for a few months and using very difficult cycling pedals/cleats on which to quickly and efficiently engage my shoes, I asked someone I considered the ultimate expert his opinion as to the best pedals available. He indicated that probably the easiest pedal to engage was the SpeedPlay Zero. He further liked the light weight—even of their heaviest models; the fact that they are user-serviceable; and that they have adjustable float.

In our house, we have six (6) racing and/or road bikes and we run SpeedPlay Zero Pedals on all of them. I cannot imagine a more efficient, easier-to-use pedal system. The company has superb customer service. I once needed a small screw to secure the grease fitting on the pedal, and SpeedPlay immediately mailed me a set.

Both Rosie and I use SpeedPlay shims under our cleats on one side due to leg-length discrepancy. I once needed screws a bit longer than the stock ones that come with the cleats. They sent those to me immediately and at no charge. For you "weight weenies", they make a titanium version and we have a few of those in use.

Checkout their whole system of adjustment products for pedals. Be sure to ask about them when you visit your favorite bike store. It goes back to being "fitted to the bike" or just getting your saddle setup. It makes a big difference in your pedal power.

Topeak JoeBlow™ Pro bicycle pump – We have owned numerous bicycle pumps, and I have had many failures and pumps that were difficult to use for one reason or another. Many of the pumps were bought so that Rosie could pump up her bike tires without having me help her. For example: We purchased a pump that was specifically for her ease of use and it had a list price of $100. It was highly rated. It was not very good. It is impossible to disengage the pump head from the tire stem without losing 10-15 psi of air. The manufacturer claimed that we must have had a faulty pump head and sent us a replacement. The result was the same. It sits in the corner of our garage.

Based upon many rave reviews, and tiring of inefficient pumps, we purchased the Topeak JoeBlow Pro™ pump. The pump is a delight to use. It is the best pump I have ever used on a valve extensions such as those on my numerous, deep- dish-carbon wheels from ZIPP™.

Topeak also has excellent customer service. A part failed on the pump head, and within two days we had a free complete replacement from the factory. We both love this pump and the customer service provided to us was appreciated greatly.

CycliStats Software – I'm a firm believer in logging every single ride with various details. This is the ultimate program with every feature that you can imagine. You can download a trial copy at www. cyclistats.com. I have logged every ride I have ever taken with this incredible software.

Guru Bicycles – There is probably no company that makes a better bicycle than the amazing Canadian company Guru. In their modern factory in Montreal, Canada, they turn out the finest custom bicycles that one can buy. The price of a custom Guru is no more than the typical off-the-shelf high-end bicycle. There is no other manufacturer that has a better fit or finish. I have two of them: a time trial bicycle— lovingly named "Jezebel" because of my attachment for her as my race-winning partner and for her flaming red and yellow custom-paint job--and my Guru "Geneo" when I want to go fast or race.

Rosie, who is less than five feet tall, has a custom "Cron'alu" time trial bike and a "Praemio" titanium road bike. Both of these bikes were specifically made for her and are the smallest frames Guru has made and they run standard wheels. Prior to purchasing another bicycle, you owe yourself a look at their incredible product line, custom built to your particular body and position.

Pearl Izumi clothing – I have yet to find better made, stylish or fitting bicycle clothing than the Pearl Izumi line of clothing and accessories. This is one company that so believes in its products that they offer an unconditional, money-back guarantee should the clothing not meet your expectations or fail you in anyway. It is not a paper guarantee – they will immediately replace any product that you return to them via mail. We have done it and it is absolutely the best customer service!

Continental Tires & Tubes – Of all the tires that I have tried and used, my absolute favorite tires for wear, ride, and performance is the Continental brand. My favorite road tires are the GP 4000 tires. They ride great, handle well, and have wear indicators on the tread. Their newest models, the so-called Black Chili versions, have lower rolling resistance and better puncture protection than previous models with no increase in weight. Although expensive, you will not find a better racing tire than the Continental Competition which comes in a 19 mm front and 22 mm rear set. I use them on my time trial bike typically pumping them up to 150 psi when the roadway is smooth.

One of the reasons that I particularly like Continental tubes is the fact that the valve in the valve stem is replaceable should you break one. I keep a collection of them by unscrewing them from tubes that are being discarded. There is a little black, plastic tool readily available that fits the flat part of the valve, or you can use a 4.5 mm wrench to remove or install a new valve.

Park Tools – Park tools is typically the tools you will find in the maintenance section of most high-end bike shops. They manufacture a complete line of quality tools for any task that the professional or garage mechanic may have. They have a wonderful website which explains the use of each tool, and has a complete section on bike maintenance.

Prolube Prolink Chain Lube – I must have tried every lube on the market. When I first purchased a bicycle, the owner of the store recommended this lube. I have to try everything in that I always want to use the best product. After using the first container, I started down the list. I find that when a chain is properly lubricated and wiped clean of extra lubricant, there is no other product that will keep your chain not only properly lubricated, but clean as well.

Pirate Gear – Sold under the brand name "PIRATE." The company produces a fantastic line of cycling clothing and accessories branded with their Pirate logo: a skull and crossbones. Based in Germany, they sell directly through a U.S. distribution channel. Not only is the clothing line extremely practical, you cannot beat the "fun factor" of wearing their clothing. I cannot get through a group ride or competition when I wear one their amazing skin suits, without positive comments and people asking me where they can buy the gear. Check them out! http://www.Pirate-hamburg.de/usmain1.htm

Zipp Wheels – There are simply no finer wheels made at the price point of a set of Zipp wheels. The Zipp 404 is great for racing and training. I time trial on a Zipp 999 set which is the 808 front and the disk rear wheel. Zipp's customer service is the best. I once raced on a course full of deep ruts which I was hitting at some rather high speeds. One of my wheels was a bit noisy after the race and neither I nor two mechanics that I brought them to could find the problem. Finally I called Zipp and they invited me to send both of my wheels back. I was totally amazed when a brand new set of two wheels arrived in the mail—and, 8,000 miles later, they are running quietly and perform like new.

Giro Helmets – I've tried numerous helmets, and I find that you cannot beat the quality or fit of the various Giro helmets. I use their road helmets and time trial helmets which and both considerably more comfortable than the two others I have owned from other manufacturers.

Cateye Strada Wireless Computer – Being an inveterate gadgeteer, an amateur radio operator, a computer hobbyist who used to build them and an engineer by schooling, I love computer stuff. I have tried all of the ones with endless bells and whistles and I now run the Cateye Wireless Strada model on my four bicycles. It is simplistic, has a large, clear readout, and works flawlessly.

Many other similar products have numerous issues like quickly going through batteries, interference, poor user friendliness, etc... This one is as straight forward as they come, and can be installed without tools. Also, for a few dollars, Cateye will sell you a second setup so that you can simply mount the same computer on two (or more) different bicycles. The computer takes only one battery as does the sensor unit. The batteries seemingly last forever.

Wippermann Chains – I love these chains. They come in different models to suit any need, they are of the highest quality, and I love their master link which can be removed and installed without use of a chain tool.

Teschner Bicycles, Teschner Technologies Group – Regarded as a 'Master Craftsman' by his peers, Teschner-built bikes are the #1 choice by many of the World's leading professional triathletes, time trialists, track and road riders. I am excited at the prospect of competing on the new, state-of-the-art Teschner 703 time trial/triathlon bike in 2010. The predecessor to the 703 won the world U23 time trial championship.

CHAPTER 28...

NUTRITION AND SUPPLEMENTATION

I hesitate to write about subjects for which I have no more than a modicum of knowledge. I am, however often asked about my diet and supplements. Apparently the catalyst for the questions is a combination of things: I have had reasonable success at racing; I do more than my share of pulling on our "A" group club rides, and win my share of sprints. Physically, I am reasonably muscular, have good vascularity and my body fat gets as low as sub 4 % when I am peaking for an event. I cannot remember the last time I had a cold or the flu.

Understand that what I describe above is not something that necessarily comes naturally to me. I have weighed as much as 198 with a 36-inch waist as an adult. I typically race at around 149 pounds with a 29-inch waist. My career is what led me to a "wellness lifestyle."

As a new hire pilot for Eastern Airlines, I would continually see notices on the pilot's lounge bulletin board bordered in black. These were announcements of the recent death of one of our pilots. I noticed that they typically died soon after the mandatory retirement age those days of 60. Another factor was that as a pilot, I was required to take an FAA, First Class physical examination every six months and an annual company physical. It didn't take much for the FAA to deny a pilot his medical certificate and, therefore, put his or her career in jeopardy. I loved my job so much and I intended to enjoy my retirement so I embarked on a plan of working out and eating properly.

Let me start with supplements in that I am asked that question rather frequently. Supplementation can be quite controversial, but I have enjoyed superior health and performance using the supplements I am about to list. Here is what I take daily:

Vitamin C	1 gram
Vitamin E	400 I.U.
Beta Carotene	15 mg
Multiple Vitamin	Puritan Pride Ultra Vita-min
Calcium	1g with 100 I.U. of vitamin D
Omega 3	1 gram
L-Lysine	500 mg
Saw Palmetto	450 mg
CO Q-10	100 mg
Garlic	500 mg
Aspirin	81 mg

I often take 3mg of melatonin about an hour prior to going to bed – I find that it makes me sleep more soundly.

Nutritionally, I try to eat a sensible diet with lots of fruits and vegetables, use skim milk rather than whole milk, whole wheat and multi-grain bread as opposed to white bread, and use one of the cholesterol-lowering spreads instead of butter.

My typical breakfast consists of a breakfast bar, a banana, and a large glass of orange juice. I will vary this with a bowl of shredded wheat and skim milk, two pieces of whole wheat toast, and a banana and orange juice on days that my training is scheduled later in the morning.

Several days a week, I do about three hours on my bike. The remainder of the week of riding begins at 6:20 AM when I leave my house and ride my bike to downtown St. Petersburg via the Pinellas Trail. I return home sometime around 12:00 Noon. I carry a Clif Bar™ with me that I consume mid-morning to help me get back home from my club rides—usually between 55-80 miles. If a particularly fast ride is planned I will often use some Clif Shot™ energy gel or Clif Shot Blocks™.

This is Rosie speaking and I would like to share some of the "secrets" of Sandy's high-energy bicycling routine and his "sensible" diet.

Lunch is a big deal especially on the long riding days and he doesn't need to worry about the calories he consumes after working out all morning—even though he weighs himself almost every day!

He arrives at the house totally out of fuel and ready to chow down on his favorite things: A roast beef sandwich on wheat with tomatoes and lettuce and pickles or smoked salmon on a bagel with capers and red onion and cream cheese, or a tuna fish sandwich. The sandwich is accompanied by baked potato chips, a mix of cashews, pecans, walnuts, and raisins, a Nutrageous™ or other peanut butter candy bar and a diet Dr. Pepper! To top it all off, he has watermelon or cantaloupe or piece of fruit and, homemade oatmeal raisin cookies, chocolate cake, or whatever delicious homemade goodie is around.

Sandy's training partner, Jerry Rush, loves to come home for lunch because there are so many goodies in the pantry. I hope you noticed and had a chuckle when I told you that he does eat baked potato chips, whole wheat bread, and drinks his diet soda…

Snacking is a big deal for Sandy. He goes through at least one large jar of peanut butter per week, helping himself to spoons full a couple of times between lunch and going to bed.

Dinner at our house is served between 6:00-6:30 PM so we have a lot of time to digest it before getting to bed early for the big rides. We both love to eat and I like to cook so we eat mostly at home. The fridge is stocked with lots of fresh fruit and veggies and we eat a lot of chicken, beef, pork, fish and pasta perhaps once a week or every other week with a salad and no protein. Every meal includes green vegetables—asparagus, spinach, and other things like that Sandy considers "esoterica"—mashed potatoes and bread for me, and a big mixed- greens and veggies salad. Of course, we usually have some dessert like frozen yogurt available because we both need to satisfy our sweet tooth!

So, eating well means eating the basic food groups. We have all been told for years to eat like our grandparents: Sticking to the tried and true works. Eat protein, complex carbohydrates including lots of fresh fruit and vegetables, beans, nuts, drink milk—if you can, and spare the caffeine and soft drinks, and drink a lot of water. That is the secret for good nutrition. After all, you see how Sandy eats and he is a real success story!

 # CHAPTER 29...

MEDICAL ISSUES FOR MASTERS ATHLETES

An Athletic Heart:

At a meeting of the European Society of Cardiology in August, 2009, experts said: "Working up a sweat may be even better than angioplasty for some heart patients…" According to the article published by the Associated Press about the meeting, Rainer Hambrecht of Klinikum Links der Weser in Bremen, Germany, published a study in 2004 that found *heart patients who rode bikes regularly were free of heart problems one year after they started their exercise regimen.* Among patients who had an angioplasty instead, only 70% were problem-free after a year." WOW!

I have been surprised by the number of heart issues that surface among some of the more accomplished masters athletes that I have known. Heart arrhythmias come in many different forms and all of them can be life-threatening even though they may seem to be benign interruptions to our bodies. We have all experienced the rather harmless phenomenon of minor arrhythmias such as an occasional missed or extra heart beat. More potentially serious and, surprisingly common, are arrhythmias such as atrial fibrillation, atrial flutter, and Supraventricular tachycardia.

I became particularly interested in the subject when I suffered an episode of atrial fibrillation some years ago. My research revealed that athletes who participate in aerobic sports tend to suffer these arrhythmias in higher percentages than non athletes who do not have diagnosed heart issues such as coronary artery disease. One of the reasons given for that phenomenon is the fact that aerobic athletes simply have more heart fibers that can go awry. I have appended a partial email that I wrote to my friend, prolific author of Wellness books, and a national and world champion athlete, Dr. Don Ardell discussing my situation:

"Don, I had a recent rather enlightening and scary experience. The late Dr. George Sheehan, world-class runner and author, on completion of a stress test in my late 30's announced that I had one of two "super hearts" that he had come across in his career as a cardiologist. The first one was a player for the NY Giants who was sent to him as a possible cardiac case, but turned out to be the best heart he had ever examined. He told me I was on a level with that guy. He told me that my airline might flag me as a heart case in that most physicians are used to seeing normal or sub-normal hearts--not super normal ones. He said that should I run into an issue on any of my required semi-annual FAA physical exams, I should refer them to him.

During a physical recently, my physician announced that I had a heart murmur and scheduled me for an echo cardiogram. He mentioned that I might have the very common mitral valve prolapse that would require taking of an antibiotic such as amoxicillin prior to any dental work. I happened to have a scheduled dental cleaning the next week and mentioned the possibility of MVP to the dentist. She decided to err on the side of caution indicating that we would reschedule the appointment when the ECO results were available. They called my physician's office and requested a copy of the report. It happened to arrive that afternoon, and I asked them to FAX me a copy. When I read the results, it prompted (2) two sleepless nights and enough research to make me an expert in reading and interpreting ECO results.

I am well aware of the athletic heart and its differences versus a normal heart and a heart enlarged for reasons like high blood pressure and other maladies. The laundry list of problems includes left ventricular hypertrophy and enlargement of the atrium. I was particularly concerned about my IVRT (isovolumetric relaxation time) which is a measure of the time in milliseconds that it takes the left ventricle to expand after pumping its load of blood through the aorta in preparation for receiving a fresh load of blood from the left atrium. Normal for someone our age (or at least over 40) is about 80 milliseconds. I recorded a time of 133 milliseconds.

During my endless research, I came upon some fascinating information. In a study of elite cyclists, there was a rather interesting study that followed the progression of left ventricular hypertrophy and thickening of the hearts walls. When this is for bad cause, it is usually indicative of diastolic dysfunction (heart not functioning well during the non-beating or diastolic stage), and often signals the beginning of what ultimately ends in heart failure.

In athletes, our hearts are able to work much harder due to the development of the muscle. The most fascinating, and, perhaps, most obscure study of all was that of elite soccer players. It was evident that this group had a mean isovolumetric relaxation time of 95 ms (normal for that group is 70 ms - anything above that is considered abnormal by the medical establishment). The control group—non-athletes-- recorded a mean reading of a normal, 78 ms.

Further research revealed that 40% of highly trained aerobic athletes will test on an ECO outside the normal range. These so-called abnormalities would be indicative of possibly serious heart problems in the general population, but speak of hearts that are superior in the aerobic athletes. About 20% will show thickening of the walls of the left ventricle or enlargement of the inside chamber.

The story is more involved, but the bottom line is that I was very concerned about my forthcoming visit to my physician. At minimum, I was expecting a referral to a cardiologist who would want to perform the gold standard test to confirm ECO results, the left ventricular and diastolic pressure test, LVEDP--an expensive, potentially dangerous, and invasive test that requires heart catheterization.

I wanted the physician to look at me in the context of who and what I am – an athlete; not just a series of numbers representative of lots of esoteric abbreviations.

I prepared my case as if I were going to present it to a jury, the decision of which would determine whether or not I would undergo heart transplantation. When he arrived in the examining room, I asked to speak first and launched into an emotional, fact-filled, extensive dissertation. I finally paused and indicated that I was ready to receive his comments. His comment was that he was well aware of my athleticism, etc., and for that reason, he was not the least concerned about the ECO results. He further mentioned that was his opinion sans my bleating. When I mature, I will learn not to fight imagined battles in lieu of sleeping--battles that rarely come to fruition."

I bring these issues up to simply make you aware of the fact that as an athlete, do not be surprised should you experience any of the arrhythmias mentioned above. I personally have suffered about one episode annually, and they seem to last for less time with each occurrence. Also, know that should you have occasion to have an Echo Cardiogram, your results will probably fall outside of the parameters considered "normal" by the medical establishment, but not be in fact abnormal readings for an aerobic athlete.

I also want to alert you to the fact that there are dangers in not discussing these arrhythmias with your physician. For example, one of the potential problems arising from the very common arrhythmia of AFIB is the fact that when the heart is in AFIB, blood tends to pool abnormally in the atrium of the heart, and when normal rhythm and blood flow is resumed there is a danger of a stroke occurring.

Also be aware of the fact that if these arrhythmias become

chronic there is rather effective treatment available. For example, my good friend, Dr. Don Ardell, who I mentioned earlier, had suffered degradation in his athletic performance. He simply could not run as fast as he had been able so to do in the recent past. A cardiology workup revealed that he was suffering from atrial flutter. He underwent a non-surgical ablation procedure.

Non-surgical ablation, used for many types of arrhythmias, is performed in a special lab called the electrophysiology (EP) laboratory. During this non-surgical procedure a catheter is inserted into a specific area of the heart. A special machine directs energy through the catheter to small areas of the heart muscle that causes the abnormal heart rhythm. This energy "disconnects" the pathway of the abnormal rhythm. It can also be used to disconnect the electrical pathway between the upper chambers (atria) and the lower chambers (ventricles) of the heart.

Dr. Ardell's procedure was so successful that he went on to win the U.S. National Sprint Triathlon, 2009, and the World Triathlon Championship, 2009, for the 70+ age group.

Dermatology:

As a poster boy for skin cancer, I am fortunate to be under the care of one of the best dermatologists in the country specializing in the treatment of skin cancer, Dr. James Connors, in St. Petersburg, FL. For a "normal" person who has undergone a surgical procedure to remove a cancerous growth, Dr. Connors typically recommends two weeks without vigorous exercise. The danger is the possibility of a hematoma forming under the sutures requiring another surgical intervention. He knows that at the most I will take one day off, so he uses the thickest possible sutures and typically does not remove them for a couple of weeks rather than the usual week. Recently, he gave me the choice of sutures or no sutures for a surgical procedure on my face. The downside of the latter choice was more scarring, but of course the former choice allowed me to train immediately. I'm sure you can guess which one was my choice! As I leave his surgical suite, Dr. Connors rolls his eyes, and hopes that he will not be seeing me to undo damage caused by exercising too soon or too vigorously. I have him well trained!

As long as I am on the subject of skin cancer, be sure to use a good broad spectrum sun block with UVA & UVB protection. Neutrogena is one favored by many dermatologists including Dr. Connors, but interestingly, one of the least expensive brands, No-Ad, comes highly recommended. I use No-Ad, and although I often ride 5 hours in the Florida sun, I do not burn my skin. Understand that my skin cancer problems are a result of many years of play in the sun during my California youth sans use of sun block.

Note that the SPF number on a sun screen product refers to the amount of protection against UVB rays; however it is vital to also have full protection against damaging UVA rays. To have that protection, your sun block must be broad spectrum and contain at least one of the following ingredients: 1) Zinc Oxide (or Titanium Dioxide, 2) Avobenzone (or Parsol 1789) 3) Mexoryl SX or 4) Helioplex which was developed by Neutrogena.

At least one of the foregoing ingredients should be at the top of the ingredient list or comprise at least 2% of the ingredients.

Consumer Research gives a Best rating to the following four products:

- Neutrogena Ultra Sheer Dry-Touch SPF55
- No-Ad SPF 45
- Blue Lizard Sun Cream Sensitive SPF 30
- Banana Boat Sport Performance Dri-Block SPF 30

If you prefer another product, check the website of the skin cancer foundation for those sun screen products that earn their seal of recommendation. Those products are listed at the following website:

www.skincancer.org/seal-of-recommendation/display.php?c=1

Too Much Wellness?

Is There Such a Thing as Too Much Wellness? This question came up as Sandy was answering a question from wellness expert, Dr. Don Ardell. Don and Sandy constantly communicate and work off one another about politics, health wellness, and sports. The final question was actually: Is there such a thing as too much wellness as it relates to our physiological efforts to become and stay elite level athletes?

Sandy was corresponding with Don about some health problems he (Don) has had for a long time but was really not paying attention to. He is a national and world champion triathlete. He went to see a doctor who prescribed some very radical medication and procedures without, Sandy considered, sufficient information. You must understand that Sandy has always wanted to be a physician and, in his very thorough and inquisitive mind, when someone needs medical treatment, he wants to make sure that they get all the answers needed and he starts researching.

Many of our friends will call Sandy and use him as a sounding board. In the past few years, he has been with me through several emergencies and surgeries. After my talks with the doctors, he has always had a list of questions to ask me that he expected me to have the answers for. NOT! There is never enough information to satisfy his intellectual curiosity. This is great because most of us get our 15 minutes with our physicians and they refer us to another doctor who may or may not give us 15 minutes before they do a procedure on you.

I am a member of the St. Pete Mad Dog Triathlon Club. Sandy has been amazed at the number of Mad Dogs, great performers in their day and still competing in their 70s and 80s, who have heart issues.

One, a world-class female triathlete in her mid-70s did a 70.3 triathlon in 2008 and underwent heart surgery in a matter of weeks after the event. Her symptoms were subtle and she just did not have the energy she normally had and her running was very tough.

Another friend, a world mountain cycling champion, national triathlete champion, track star, swimmer, and bicycle racer who just turned 80, felt great and had his annual checkup and the doctor told him he had to have a pacemaker put in! His heart rate was somewhere around 36 beats per minute which was normal for him because it would go up when he was exercising—which is mostly every day.

Matt Bostic, a 21 year old athlete, died while having a friendly race with a friend at work also sudden cardiac arrest. Recently, well-known triathlete and Iron Man winner, Steven Larsen, died at the age of 39 while on a training run with other elite athletes.

Dr. Don Ardell publishes a weekly Wellness newsletter called The Ardell Wellness Report. Here is a letter to the editor that Sandy recently submitted with Don's answer:

"Don - I have broached this subject with you before, but a recent revelation has me in the research mode. The question I posed basically related to the high number of athletes who seem to have medical issues - especially heart related issues and cancer."

"I'm a national class age group cyclist who trains on the bicycle about 27 hours a week. In addition to that, I supplement my aerobic exercise with weight training 2-3 times a week. I associate with many hard-core athletes who train a similar amount of time."

"I am struck by the number of heart-related issues, such as Atrial Fibrillation, Atrial Flutter and Supraventricular Tachycardia suffered by this apparently very healthy group (certainly from the perspective of appearance and athletic performance)."

"There also seems to be a more than normal number of cancers. For example, one of the group was recently diagnosed with metastasized melanoma and another with pancreatic cancer. Both exercise much more than the norm and compete regularly. There have been quite a few cases of prostate cancer among the elite athletes."

"I am beginning to wonder if those of us who exercise to the extreme are actually more likely to suffer maladies of the heart and cancer."

"I am aware of the fact that athletic hearts tend to suffer more arrhythmias than the normal population due apparently to the extra heart fibers that can go awry. I am arguably one of the best over 65 year old cyclists in the United States. However, I suffer an occasional bout of AFIB—something I never experienced until well ensconced in my ridiculously high number of hours that I spend training every week. Is there a story here?"

"Perhaps the cancer tie-in is an issue of free radicals out of control. Is there a study regarding athletes such as myself versus people who do exercise, but not to extremes, in regards to the likelihood of developing heart issues and/or cancer?"

"Perhaps the issue is simply exposure - I tend to more intimately know and hang out with athletes. Perhaps if I hung out with the white underbelly types, the picture would seem even more ghastly. Am I just chasing my tail, or is there a tale here?"

Response from Don Ardell:
"Sandy - Let's assume for just a moment that over-the-top competitive be the best you can be exertions day in and day out over the years, particularly the senior years, cause all the heart and other hazards identified in your excellent post."

"Would you cut back, do less and slide into life's peloton? I'm going out on a limb here - I'd wager the answer is, No, you would not. If the risk is higher, it's one most of us would take with eyes wide open."

"Being dead can't be that bad, anyway, and being really alive as long as possible at full power seems the way to go. Good cheer."

Dr. Ardell was correct as to what my answer would have been, but I do find it an intriguing subject. However I have not come to any conclusions regarding this "issue."

LDL Pattern "B" Blood Type:

LDL Pattern "B" is a Common, but little known cause of Sudden Cardiac Arrest (SCA) in athletes of all ages.

Robert Ray, my deceased husband, died of Sudden Cardiac Arrest (SCA) while swimming a regular, Tuesday evening swim with the St. Pete Mad Dog Triathlon club. He had no coronary heart disease. He was healthy and an active triathlete. No one expected him to die. When they did the autopsy, it showed no reason for his death. All that they could surmise was that it was due to a blood clot in a small artery caused by a flake of plaque that dislodged and caused his heart to stop. A defibrillator at the pool could have possibly saved his life. But there was none there.

LDL patterns "A" and "B" refer to the size of the LDL particles in the blood. LDL Pattern B is the mysterious cause of many heart attacks in men. Robert and many other men, in particular, are on statin drugs to take care of their cholesterol. With LDL pattern B, the medication does its job in the big arteries but not in the smaller ones.

After Robert's death, his older brother who had a quadruple bypass with aorta valve replacement at age 52 was asked to take a blood test for LDL pattern "B" by his cardiologist. The test is only run at Berkeley Life Science Lab in CA. When the results came back, Barton Ray was shown to have this type of blood. It is very prevalent in families where there is a history of high cholesterol and triglycerides, high blood pressure, strokes, heart attacks and Sudden Cardiac Arrest. According to a study done by the National Dairy Council, 20%-30% of the U.S. population has genetically-influenced LDL pattern "B." It is particularly prevalent in men but is also inherited by women.

The smaller, fewer HDL particles do not clean up the smaller, denser, and stickier LDL particles that can clog up the small arteries. There is a tendency for the small arteries to vibrate and, because the small HDL particles do not clean them up, they flake and cause blood clots. This stops the heart or puts it into arrhythmia—an alteration in the rhythm of the heartbeat either in time or force.

LDL pattern "A" which most of us have is large, buoyant LDL particles that do not get into the smaller arteries as a normal case of event. The HDL of pattern "A" are large and many and do a terrific job of cleaning up the bad cholesterol in the major arteries.

If you have a history in your family of sudden cardiac arrest and all of the other symptoms, your family members should be tested for LDL pattern "B." Lifestyle changes can make a difference in the LDL pattern you have.

Check out the Internet for a lot of information on this blood condition. It could save your life or that of someone in your family.

Illustrations: C1, C2 & Other Vertebrae

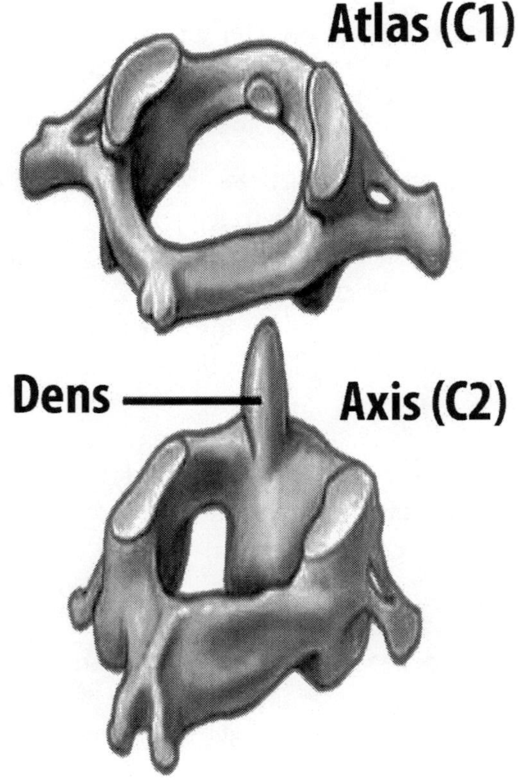

With respect to the cervical spine two areas can be differentiated:

The Atlas (C1) as shown is the "broken neck" that Sandy suffered. Note that it actually sits atop the Dens—the Axis. the top with two vertebrae - Atlas and Axis (see diagram 1) o   the lower section with the next 5 vertebrae

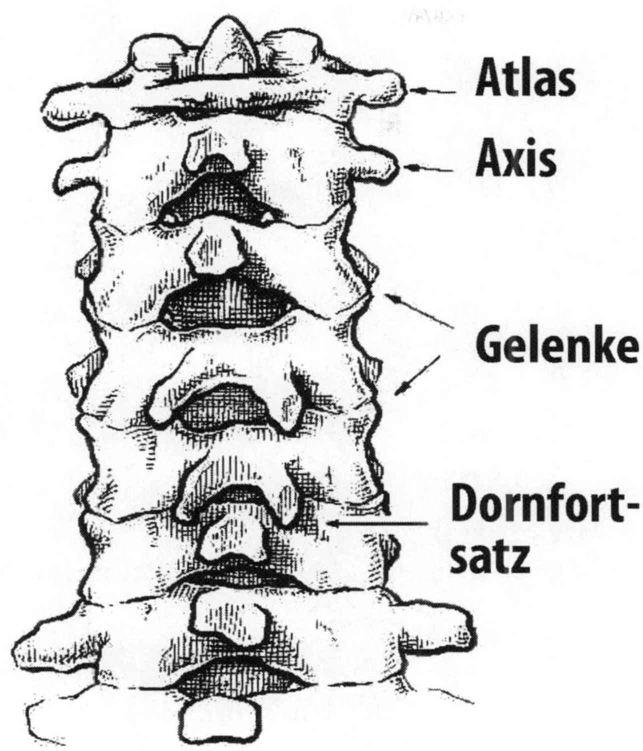

Diagram 1 ***Cervical Spine -View from the rear***

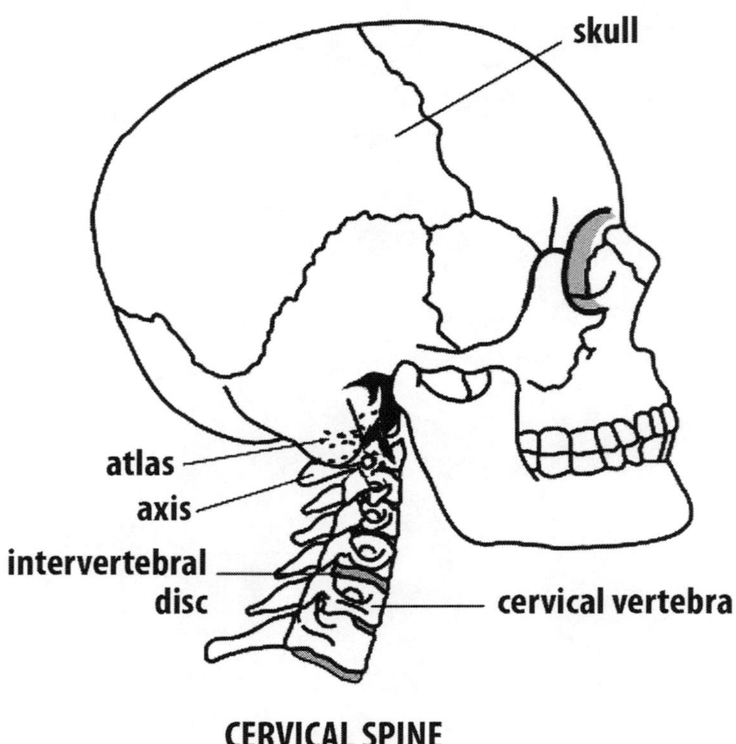

CERVICAL SPINE

Bone: Atlas (anatomy)

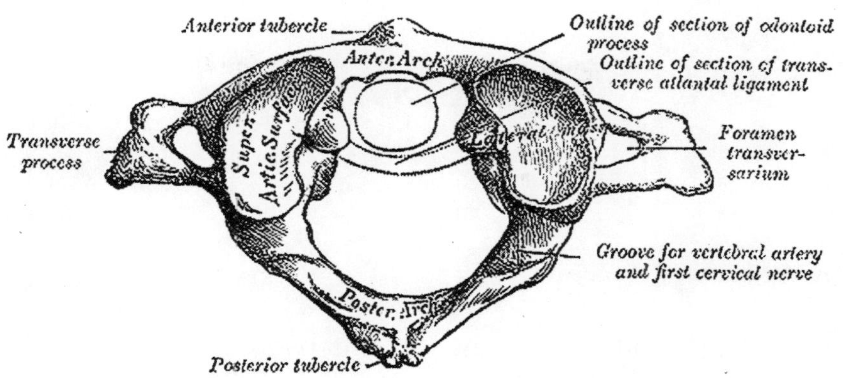

First cervical vertebra, or Atlas

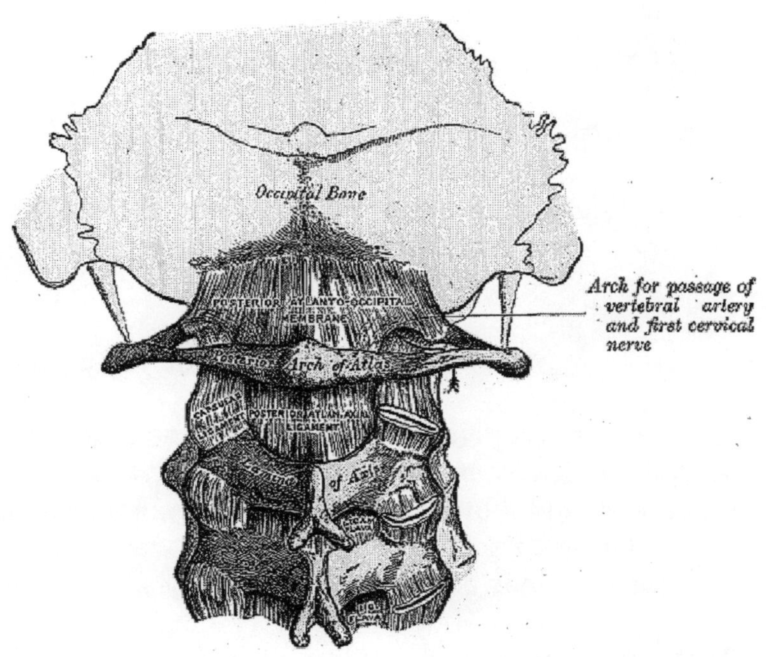

Posterior atlantoöccipital membrane and atlantoaxial ligament.
(Atlas visible at center.)

CHAPTER 30...

ANECDOTES

Kitty Hawk Interview

Kitty Hawke and Sandy Scott: Kitty Interview by Kris DiGiovanni, a free-lance writer Sandy met in our local dog park. She was interested in the similarities between our builds and asked if she could write a story from Kitty's point of view.

"Pets and Their People: Love at First Sight for Two Retired Runners"
Posted by Kris DiGiovanni, Published: January 10, 2009

"Today I'm interviewing a retired racing Greyhound, WJS Kittyhawk, who owns Sandy Scott, a retired cross-country racer and champion cyclist.

Me: So, Kitty… May I call you Kitty? I understand you used to race.

Kitty: All my friends call me Kitty, so certainly, go ahead. In fact, it really freaks people out when my human calls, "Here, Kitty, Kitty," and a 60-pound Greyhound shows up. But to answer your question, yes, I raced at three different tracks, and girlfriend, I was fast. In 83 races, I was in the money 43 times, and finished first 13 times.

Me: That's pretty impressive, but I hear you are an ex-con. What's up with that?

Kitty: Yes, it's true. When I hung up my racing muzzle, I needed something else to do. I ended up in prison, at the Lakeland Correctional Facility in Michigan. There's a program there sponsored by The National Greyhound Foundation called Second Chance at Life. It matches up retired greyhounds and prison inmates. We spent three months teaching them the basics: compassion, responsibility, and love - and in return they show(ed) us how to sit, stay, heel, etc. It works out pretty well.

Me: So how did you hook up with your human? Kitty: Beverly Sebastian, founder of the NGF, told me about a man who was looking for a fast friend – cat and small dog friendly, sweet, girly girl and of course that's me to a "T". So she suggested Sandy Scott. I have to admit that when I first saw him it was like looking at my "brother from another mother." He's lean and lanky, like me, has a pale complexion, a little grey around the muzzle. It was definitely love at first sight. The clincher was he's an ex-runner too.

Me: A runner, you say?

Kitty: We'll, he's retired from that now, but back in the day, he ran a fair amount. He held the National Championship in the 10,000 meter cross country, the 5000 meter, and the 4x1 mile relay. I can beat him out of the blocks every time, but he can smoke me in the stretch. I'm a sprinter after all.

Me: So you two run together?

Kitty: Nope. I'm retired. But a girl has to keep her figure. I take him to the dog park pretty much every day so I can keep up my exercise routine. It's only fair, since he spends all morning on his bike.

Me: Aha, so he's a cyclist?

Kitty: Not just "a cyclist," he's got over ten Florida State Championships and holds every state record in his age group….

Me: You must be so proud.

Kitty: Well, I am and I'm not. The guy's not too bright. A few years ago he swerved to avoid an official during a race and went right over the handle bars. Broke his neck at C-1. You'd think he'd learn a lesson. But no, within a week he was back on a trainer, and in 2007, darned if he didn't win the AMS Masters Comeback of the Year Award. He still rides an average of 50 miles a day, and competes regularly.

Me: Sounds like a pretty determined athlete.

Kitty: Well, he's always had that "Top Gun" personality, you know, the "need for speed?" He started out as a motorcycle cop in California. ….He got his pilot's license and flew for Eastern Airlines for more than 25 years….He finally retired from the rat race, but just couldn't keep still. He took up cycling at 64, and hasn't looked back. He just got a blogging gig at HYPERLINK "http://www.masters-athlete.com/" "Masters Athlete Magazine." <u>Master Athlete</u>.

Me: So, Kitty, it sounds like you have a pretty good life now.

Kitty: I can't complain. I've got Sandy pretty well trained now. His fiancé's Lab-mix, Sasha, and I get along great, even though she does tend to get a bit hoggish with her ratty tennis balls. (Between you and me, they don't really taste that good anyway.) I've got lots of buds at the dog park, and a snazzy custom collar. Life is good.

Me: So how can other humans find great greyhound companions like you?

Kitty: Well, of course there's the <u>**Second Chance at Life Program,**</u> **but in the Tampa Bay area, there are two rescue agencies, <u>GREAT</u>,**

and <u>Greyhound Pets of America</u>. Just check them out on the Web and they will hook you up. Of course all three organizations could always use donations, so if you're not looking to get adopted by a dog just yet, you can still help out.

Me: Thanks, Kitty; it's been great talking with you. See you around the dog park.

Kitty: You're welcome, and Wooof!

Bill Shafer

In response to the interview with Ms. Kitty Hawke: Contributed by Bill Shafer, GrowingBolder.com

"Thank you for the tip on your very interesting interview. You're to be commended, not just for your work in helping rehabilitate prisoners, but the much more difficult and exceptional job you've done keeping Sandy Scott out of trouble. Why, I haven't seen his name in an accident report in several years! And whatever you've done to keep him motivated, well, I wish you'd share that with the rest of us. Every time I read that you have him riding for an average of 50 miles per day, it really does make me want to double down on my efforts to stay as active as possible. Thank you so much, Kitty for what you've done. You've helped Sandy become one of the most fun, interesting, uplifting, inspiring and motivating people I've ever heard of. He may not realize it all the time, but he's changing lives, just from his example! So tonight, be sure to add a little extra kibble into his food bowl! Oh, and thanks so much for letting him keep Growing Bolder, too!"

Dr. George Sheehan

In the 1980s, Dr. George Sheehan was a friend, prolific author, cardiologist, medical editor for *Runner's World*, and my teammate on the Shore AC. I once had the joy of pacing him to an American age group record for 1500 meters at the Northeastern Regional AAU championships at Princeton University. Although he was a busy cardiologist, if you were a friend and wanted to discuss anything running related, he would happily take your telephone call during business hours at his very busy cardiology practice in Red Bank, NJ. I was having constant pains in a certain part of my upper leg, and I called George at work and said, "I have continual pain in my Pectineus, what can I do about it?" George's reply was, "What the hell is a Pectineus?" to which I replied, "It's a muscle in the upper leg - I got the anatomical term for the muscle from the *Encyclopedia of Athletic Medicine*, written by Dr. George Sheehan! We had a great laugh.

CHAPTER 31...

THE FINISH LINE

Looking back through the book to both Sandy Scott and Dave Viney, two outstanding masters athletes, you should be saying, "I can do that too!" All of the information that you need to get to work and on your way to winning the gold is in this book

The simple truth is that there are more people becoming involved in competitions and the United States Senior Games every year. There were 12,000 masters athletes at the National Senior Games in Louisville, KY, 2007. In 2009, there were approximately 12,750 attendees in San Francisco—even with the recession. The next games will be in Houston in 2011 and you need to get ready to be there with your bike. If you cannot make it to Houston, perhaps you can make Cleveland in 2013. As a note:

- Approximately 30,000 athletes qualified to be in the Senior Olympics—just the top two contenders.

- Here in Florida, 2000 Athletes competed in the State of Florida 2008 Senior Games championship.

- Over a period of 15 years of Senior Games championships in the State of Florida, 30,857 athletes have competed.

There are many opportunities to compete if you have the interest and you can combine your cycling with running, track and field, for tennis—whatever suits your particular athletic interests. When you take a vacation to ski country, you can participate in the Senior Games' skiing, snowboarding, and other winter sports' events. It does not matter that you are a resident in another state or that it is not cycling weather. Perhaps you can convince a group of friends to get together a couple of times per week and take a long bike ride—or start a local bicycling club.

Sandy and I hope that you enjoyed the book and recommend it to your friends that are couch potatoes. The old saying, "If you don't use it, you lose it" certainly holds true as many studies have shown. I am traveling to Connecticut for my 50th class reunion. I have printed out a half-dozen maps from www.MapMyRide.com. The selected rides around Fairfield County vary from three to 31 miles—some of them are on roads I used to ride as a child with my sister, Pat. It is a terrific source of information for those of us who travel and like to take our bikes along for our exercise. Between the maps and a GPS, you can go anywhere your heart takes you.

Rosie racing to the finish - 10K Time Trial at the U.S. Senior Games Nationals, Senior Olympics, 08/09. - Bob Butsic, Photographer

 # CHAPTER 32...

ABOUT THE AUTHOR

Rose Marie Ray was born and raised in Norwalk, Connecticut to a large, Italian-American family. She and her four sisters were encouraged to participate in sports by their father, a semi-pro athlete. He provided them with the best sports equipment in their neighborhood, including a basketball court, softball and hardball gloves and bats, golf clubs, skates, rackets, et al, and took them to wrestling and boxing matches, football and baseball games with "the guys." Rosie enjoyed sports her entire life especially swimming, roller and ice skating, water and snow skiing, softball, tennis, golf, track, squash, racket ball, and basketball, and, of course, bicycling.

In 1961, she moved to Boston, MA, where she began a career in the computer industry with Honeywell Information Systems. Starting as an executive secretary/technical writer of programmer manuals, she advanced through programming and systems analysis and design to become the only woman in sales worldwide based in New York City.

In 1975, after being laid off out of seniority and with a big contract for a large French bank in her hands, she filed a case with the State of New York for equal opportunity for all women who were denied job opportunities at Honeywell, Inc. The case was conciliated in her favor and set a precedent that holds to this day.

She moved to Dallas, Texas, with her husband, Robert, and two children, Pamela and Ian. She was a successful sales executive in Dallas between 1977 and 1992 where she worked with three (3) major computer companies including several more years with Honeywell after its acquisition of a company she was working for in 1977.

In 1991, as a result of her experiences of breaking the glass ceiling for woman as a high-powered women in sales and marketing, mother, and homemaker, she wrote a successful "how to" book for women in transition: *SuperWomen Do IT Less…..A guide to having it all: children, a career, and a loving relationship.* She was chosen as "Speaker In Residence" for Texas Woman's University in 1992, and enjoyed speaking engagements where she could motivate women to realize their potential in life as a careerist, wife, and mother.

In 1996, after finishing up her college degree in business and management information systems, Rosie retired to St. Petersburg, FL, where she and Robert owned and operated a successful bed and breakfast inn. In 2002, the inn was put on the market after the death of Robert from sudden cardiac arrest.

In 2005, she sold the B&B and retired to pursue her cycling and triathlon training while working as a consultant to the hospitality industry. She is the State of Florida, 2009, USCF Women Over 60 years, 20K time trial champion and the USGA 40K road race champion and represented the State of Florida at the U.S. Senior Games' Senior Olympics in 2007 and 2009.

Rosie writes from her home in Seminole, Florida and is a member of the St. Pete Mad Dogs Triathlon Club, and Chair of the Board of the St. Pete Mad Dogs Charities, the St. Pete Bicycle Club, and National Association of Female Executives.

Base & Strength Building 68, 69.
basic metabolic rate 80.
bench press 82, 83, 84.
bicycle 52, 53, 54, 57, 58.
bicycle frame 53.
bike. *See* bicycle.
Bill Shafer. *See* Shafer.
BMR. *See* basic metabolic rate.
Bostic 177.
brake hoods 157.
break-away 8.
breathing squat. 85.
Brooks 90.
Burk 131.
Burke 30.

C

C-1 26. *See also* vertebra.
caffeine 108.
Calf Raises 86.
Callahan 2.
capillarisation 89, 91.
carbohydrates 156.
carbon wheels 162.
Cardiac Arrest 179, 180. *See also* heart attacks.
cardiologist 60.
Carr 157.
Cateye 164, 165.
Cervelo 56.
cervical vertebra 184.
Chain Wear 151.
championship 154.
chiropractic 22.
cholesterol 179, 180.
Chris Scott. *See* Scott.
Chronic Back 157.
club rides 166, 167.
coaching 10.
cog 110.
Cole 22.
competition 47.

Dr. Rhonda Schroeder. *See* Rhonda Schroeder.

K

L

M

pipe cleaners 154.
Piper's patients. *See* Dr. Mark Piper's.
Pirate Gear 164.
Plantar fasciitis 6.
Polar Heart Rate Monitor™ 45.
polka dot jersey 119.
power meter 155.
Pre-race meal 107.
Prolube 163.
protein 168, 169.
pump 106.
punctures 110.

R

race number 53.
Race of Truth 104.
race-pace pickups 109.
Race Preparation 106.
race venue 109.
radiologists 33.
Rainer Hambrecht of Klinikum. *See* Hambrecht.
ramp start 110.
Ray 155.
rear-wheel disk 53.
records 60.
Recovery Pulse Index 101.
repetitions 111.
Rest and Recovery 68.
rest interval 126.
Rhonda Schroeder 36.
Rivera 103.
road race 104, 116.
Roger Banister. *See* Banister.
Roger Burke. *See* Burke.
Rotational weight 150.
routine 157.
Rows 86.
Runner's World 128.
Rush 123.

S

supplements 166.
Supraventricular tachycardia 170.
surgeons 1.
sweet spot 58.

T

tactics 119, 120.
tailwind 110.
tapering 70.
technical course 115.
Teschner 165.
The Perry Rader Squat System 85.
tire pump 106.
tire stem 161.
tire tape 150.
Tom Danielson. *See* Danielson.
tool kit 106.
Topeak 161, 162.
training 164.
triathletes 165.
triglycerides 180.
tubular tires 55, 56.
Tubular Tires 150.
turn around 113.

U

UCI World Cycling Championships 50.
United States Cycling Federation 50.
University of Pennsylvania 27.
USCF. *See* United States Cycling Federation.

V

valve stem 148, 149.
Van Courtland Park 128, 129.
vascularity 166.
ventricular hypertrophy 172.
vertebra 26.
Vertebrae 181.
Viney 190.
VO2max 71.

W

Y

Z